Michael Anthony lives in Vancouver, British Columbia; he received an MBA in International Management from Asia Pacific International University, 16 April 1993.

His interests include acting on stage, commercials, films, and golf. "We cannot continue to live the way we do; we must change."

This work has been inspired by Sadhguru, his dedication to planting millions of trees in India to save the soil. You will find many of his wisdom and words throughout this work.

We need many more of his kind on this planet. Also, want to thank Michel Montpetit.

To Sophia,

ALWAYS Show LOVE &COMPASSION FOR ALL LIVING THINGS& EACh OTHER.

G. Anthony

Michael Anthony

Conscious (R)Evolution, Humanity, Insanity, and the Planet

Austin Macauley Publishers™

LONDON • CAMBRIDGE • NEW YORK • SHARJAH

Ordering Information
Quantity sales: Special discounts are available on quantity purchases by corporations, associations, and others. For details, contact the publisher at the address below.

Publisher's Cataloging-in-Publication data
Anthony, Michael
Conscious (R)Evolution, Humanity, Insanity, and the Planet

ISBN 9798886937374 (Paperback)
ISBN 9798886937381 (Hardback)
ISBN 9798886937398 (ePub e-book)

Library of Congress Control Number: 2023919200

www.austinmacauley.com/us

First Published 2024
Austin Macauley Publishers LLC
40 Wall Street, 33rd Floor, Suite 3302
New York, NY 10005
USA

mail-usa@austinmacauley.com
+1 (646) 5125767

I would like to thank all the people at Austin Macauley Publishers for their belief in a new way of living on this planet, to all their staff and production crew for their hard work to getting this publication on the market.

Table of Contents

Prolog

No species has had such a wholesale control over everything on earth, living or dead as we now have, that lays upon us awesome responsibilities. In our hands lies not only our own future, but that of all other living creatures with whom we share the earth. David Attenborough Life on Earth.

Somewhere in the world there is a little boy or girl, perhaps five or six years old playing with little friends not knowing that today's adults will decide what their future will look like.

By the time they graduate from university, the decision world leaders make concerning global carbon emissions now will ultimately and drastically alter the world environment they live in.

Man has been endowed with reason, with the power to create, so that he can add to what he's been given. But he hasn't been a creator, only a destroyer. Forests keep disappearing, rivers dry up, wild life has become extinct, the climate's ruined and the land grows poorer and uglier every day.

Anton Chekhov, Uncle Vanya, 1897.

We all know it; we all know what is coming if we continue down the path that humanity has chosen. The real question is why we continue relentlessly, knowing in our hearts the end result will not end well for our future generations.

Why? What will be the outcome for continued un-relentless economic growth? The future is certain yet we continue to deny our future and our children's future. Why?

The world is in turmoil, we lost our way, global warming, pollution, plastics in the oceans, forests disappearing, and environmental destruction in the name of economic growth and profits and greed. Greed will be the death of humanity. We are on a path of self-destruction. The planet is choking, we are in a crisis, but yet world governments have no sense of urgency.

The magnificence of mountains, the serenity of nature— nothing is safe from the idiot marks of man's passing. Loudon Wainwright.

We are vested in the here and now, what can I do for myself now. We work all of our lives to a job that enslaves us with the benefits of pay to enhance and ease our lives with comfort. Most of these jobs involve the raping or poisoning the planet in some way.

Let me reveal the paths we are on; we have all seen it yet we continue to live in denial. What is it all about? The endless pursuit of money, wealth, power, pleasure, more conveniences just to make our lives easier? We are constantly being suffocated to be and to get something more all the time. When will we settle and say what I have is sufficient, to live and enjoy life? The whole of humanity wants the American dream to expand our unrealistic expectations to expand in an ever-limitless economic expansion. Our existence has become the parasites on this planet. Our own intelligence has turned against us. Our expectations change yearly, expecting more and more. We are in a war with the planet, consuming more than what is necessary to live, we are on a binge of exploitation, consuming more and more, this cannot end well.

We have lost our way, we have lost touch with our reality, and we do not recognize other lives other than our own egotistic selves. We have created an illusory madness. We have lost our common sense. Our future is at stake, how can we put a price on that?

If we know it beforehand and let it happen, is it not a crime of the worst kind? The awareness is within us, but we have not yet developed the consciousness necessary for humanities survival on this planet. If we continue to let our past become our future, there will be no future. We must break this cycle by developing our conscious reality.

Everyone is in a state of dementia. Every time we travel on this path it looks new. People tell us it is better; but it is the same. It feels like we are being led somewhere, but we are going nowhere. We are going in circles. We are repeating the past; the past is the anchor that prevents us from getting where we need to go. We do not have to go and search for the truth it is directly in front of us. Like the ominous sword of Damocles, hanging above our collective heads. Those who can make positive change on our planet have the most vested interests in changing nothing. Because they are trapped in the economic growth which has improved the living conditions of a small minority but will devastate the lives of the future. They make insignificant decisions on the real reality of our situation. We think the planet is a bottomless pit of resources, the oceans are infinite, the air will last forever the water will nourish us forever. We must not let our industries monopolize the use of water for their use and consume water for their production processes. Water will be urgently required for all life.

But; look at the reality, where are we?

What is the end if not the destruction of all life, when will the lesson be learned?

"Human kind has not woven the web of life. We are but one thread within it. Whatever we do to the web, we do to ourselves. All things are bound together. All things connect." – Chief Seattle 1855.

Chapter 1
Why Should I Be Concerned

Economy

It does not stop there. We produce consumer goods endlessly measuring a countries wealth by economic growth. Let me share some startling data—100 million cars produced each year pumping CO_2 in the atmosphere causing climate change no it is a climate catastrophe.

Gas Exploration, Industrial farming, burning coal and fossil fuels, deforestation, plastic disposal, atomic energy disposal, product obsolescence, packaging, global transportation, water pollution, filling in swamps, lakes and seas, pipelines, tar sands, toxic chemicals, no or ineffective re-cycling, ALL IN THE NAME OF A GROWING ECONOMY.

Let me state categorically economic growth is absolutely the wrong measure. The countries wealth is the measure of healthy environments. If countries used this measure, all human beings would live healthy lives with a bounty of nature to eat from and live in. A world that needs billions of products to be made needs to produce a massive amount of energy. The unbridled economic growth without taking environmental consequences into measure will cause the death of all of us.

Water

I would not normally talk of water, water was so plentiful. It was free we could drink from the streams and from the wells. With global warming, fresh water will become a very precious commodity. The U.N. is warning of draining humanity's lifeblood and worsening water scarcity. "We are draining humanities lifeblood through overconsumption and unsustainable use and evaporating it through global heating."

"In Africa, 82 million face acute hunger and famine due to drought and eradicating hunger is unattainable without water. Corporations and global drinks companies are operating in water stressed places. Shame on us. Corporations pump so much groundwater out of the ground into plastic bottles, there is not enough for agriculture. Privatization of water is a catastrophe in the making." U.N General Secretary Antonio Guterres.

"Access to water and sanitation is a fundamental human right, and that personal and domestic needs must take priority over industrial use and profits." The water Justice manifesto by Pedro Arrojo. (U.N.)

Pepsi co, chief sustainability Officer stated that half the world will face water scarcity as soon as 2025. "Water scarcity and insecurity will become the world's greatest crisis. Globally more than 2 billion people lack access to safe drinking water and over 4 billion people experience severe water scarcity. Ref: Fortune, Jim Andrew."

Why? Humanity caused global warming. We caused it. We can through global consciousness stop our own insanity.

Fertilizers

We use chemical fertilizers that do not stay in the fields, the fertilizers run into the streams and rivers and into ocean causing bloom which choke the oxygen and cause enormous dead zones. Dead Zones are areas of the bottom of the waters where oxygen is too depleted to support life. Synthetic fertilizers are composed mostly of nitrogen and phosphorous. They promote quick growth in farms or in your garden yet the damage to the soil is enormous. These fertilizers cause algae blooms which choke the water of oxygen and nothing lives in the water where there are enormous amounts of bloom. These areas are seriously affected when all the nitrates come out of the Rivers, and flow into the gulf. Heavy metal contaminants, like cadmium, and mercury found in some synthetic fertilizers find their way into our food supplies. All these chemicals then enter our bodies with disastrous health consequences. Fertilizers contain nitrous oxide that is carried into the waterways and evaporates into the atmosphere. Nitrous oxide is another cause of global warming with methane and carbon dioxide.

There are now over 405 identified dead zones worldwide including the Baltic Sea, parts of the East and south Coast of the US and several west coast outlets, there is a dead zone at the mouth of the Mississippi river that runs into the Gulf of Mexico. The Gulf of Mexico is being choked to death. (Ref: The Guardian.com/environment, Aug 2021)

Chemicals Paints, Oils

Fruit companies, as an example, use chemicals at almost every stage of the growth process. Chemical fertilizers to keep the soil fertile, herbicides to keep the growing area vegetation free, nematicides to protect roots from damage, fungicides to prevent damaging fungi. Inside the bodies of Americans are more than 200 chemicals including at least six carcinogens according to the Center for Disease Control and Prevention. US Manufacturers are not required to demonstrate that their chemicals are safe. Chemicals are produced endlessly regardless of consequence to the planet.

How did we reach this point? What insanity.

When some high-sounding institute states that a compound is harmless or a process is risk free, it is wise to know from where the institute or the scientists obtain their financial support.

Then we ask where have all the river fish gone? How could we have let this happen?

Water, water, water everywhere and not a drop to drink. The culprit is chemicals, paints, varnishes, thinners, oils, that disappear down drain storms never to be seen again, toxic pollution causes irreparable environmental damage time and time again. Repeat this scenario in every village, every town, every city across the world and what do you have? When will we stop?

In the last 30 years, our chemical poisons have poisoned insects of all kinds. These insects are nutrients for birds and animals and their bodies provide nutrients to the soil. We in turn poison the birds and animals we love from poisoned insects. Can we not see the interconnection of life? These insects that eat our crops are also important for the life of the soil when in their short lives they die.

"Civilization wrecks the planet from seafloor to stratosphere." – Richard Bach

If any oil, gas, or chemical spills in water on the top of the ground, this contamination will travel miles, it does not rest it does not stop. It travels 44 miles per day, whichever way the water travels. Contaminated ground water will eventually discharge and merges back to the land to surface into rivers and oceans. A pint of oil can cover an acre of a lake; 1 gallon of gas can contaminate 750,000 gallons of water (Data from Waterfacts) It is not the only culprit. Septic tanks, chemicals of all sorts, road salt, atmospheric contaminants, fertilizers, pesticides, all contaminate ground water and leads to the erosion of plants and the dying-off of animal species. Did you know last year 1.7 million pounds of insecticides were applied to over 1.3 million acres of California farmland containing PFAS, far exceeding what the EPA considers safe in drinking water. (Data Center for Biological Diversity May 2023) Multiply this by every state, country and nation we are slowly contaminating ourselves.

We must ban all chemicals. Chemical companies are guilty unless proven innocent, no more "proprietary" bullshit.

Go and watch Dark Waters a 2019 film about Dupont Chemicals, based on a true story of our sad state of affairs.

"For the first time in the history of the world, every human being is now subjected to contact with chemicals, from the moment of conception till death." – Rachel Carson, Silent spring 1962.

Gas and Fracking

Gas exploration; what a good idea, we will extract gas by pressurizing shale deposits in the ground to produce energy and we will call it fracking. How is this pressurization accomplished? Hundreds of deadly chemicals are used and pumped into the ground along with massive amount of water. *The EPA identified **1,084 different chemicals** reported as used in fracking formulas between 2005 and 2013. Common ingredients include methanol, ethylene glycol, and propargyl alcohol. Those chemicals, along with many others used in fracking fluid, are considered hazardous to human health. Apr 19, 2019.*

What is Fracking? Hydraulic fracturing blasts water and chemicals 8,000 ft into the ground and under intense pressure breaks up the shale rock and release the gases. Seems harmless? Fracking fluid contains over 596 different chemicals such as (TCMTB) and other unknown proprietary chemicals whose names you cannot even pronounce. Glycol ethers a known carcinogen causes among other things embryo malformation, bone marrow disease, hemolysis a destruction of red blood cells. 1 well requires 1 to 7 million gallons of water, and a well can be fracked up to 18 times in its existence. Of All the water that goes down only 50% of it comes back into huge pits to hold it. Evaporation sprayers are used to reduce the size of the water pits and are sprayed in the air to evaporate; it contains the toxins that were sent underground and then puts them in the atmosphere to return to earth as toxic rain. 70% of fracking fluids remain in the ground and are not bio-degradable. (Ref: What is fracking and why is it controversial, BBC, Oct. 2022)

In 1972, Nixon signed a clean air act. In 2005, the energy bill introduced by Dick Cheney (CEO of Halliburton a major supplier of fracking fluids (Hazardous chemicals) to the energy industry) exempts the Oil and Gas industry from the clean water act. A loophole in 2005 US energy Bill exempts gas drillers (called fracking) from EPA guidelines such as the Clean Water Act. (Web of Entanglement).

These gas well are all over the US particularly **Texas, Oklahoma, New Mexico, Wyoming, and Louisiana**, and different provinces of Canada like BC. The end result has not yet reared its ugly head. The end result is ground water contamination, water pollution, destruction of land, wild life and fishery, cancers of various kinds, chemicals that do not bio-degrade and worst of all water flows underground to rivers that are interconnected. To a world that is interconnected. Water wells are polluted, we need clean water, and we can't drink oil and gas. The water wells have been drinkable for hundreds of years, any well near gas fracking operations stink of turpentine and cannot be drunk, because they are now polluted. I have seen water coming out of taps easily set on fire with a match. Fracking companies have used more than 282 million pounds of hazardous chemicals from 2014 to 2021. (Ref: published in Environmental Pollution).

Are we insane?

"We never know the value of water till the well is dry."
– Thomas Fuller, Gnomologia 1732.

Unfortunately it is no longer dry it is polluted.

"Oh the web we weave, humanity and its insanity."

The average fracking job uses **roughly 4 million gallons of** water per well—or about as much water as New York City uses every six minutes. (Ref: Data.API.org.) Oh, by the way, the world is running out of natural water. Poisoning the water underground, because water does not stop where it is, water knows no boundaries, it goes everywhere and will carry the poison with it. Farmers that have been withdrawing water from their wells for hundreds of years and now can no longer use their own wells.

The energy that is produced by these gases goes where? It is converted into greenhouse gases that trap the hot air in the atmosphere, which results in global warming. Did you know 20 billion dollars are the US subsidies given for fossil fuel industries in the year 2020? (data provided by Environmental Energy and Study Institute Mar. 2022) Will we continue to subsidize global warming? Have we gone mad? Global warming is upon us, yet we continue to burn fossil fuels to keep industry going, driving our cars to go to work. Yet the planet is burning up. Can we not see? Our world is on fire, we cannot run away from our future.

Only man can use poison to extract gas. It is insanity at the highest level and governments allow it.

"Your grandchildren will likely find it incredible—or even sinful—that you burned up a gallon of gasoline to fetch a pack of cigarettes" – Paul MacCready Jr.

Pesticides

We are losing our bee population they are important for farmers to pollinate crops without the bees the plants lose their production. We have robbed bees of their rich food source by cutting down the environment to a single huge farm of one plant, say corn. It is like you eating only corn for the rest of your life how good is that? Then we introduce tons of pesticides to the farm to get rid of pests again we lose the bees, now we lose the birds because they eat the bugs that died because of the pesticide and the birds are poisoned. Nature is an endless chain whatever chain we as intelligent beings want to stop, will have serious repercussion to elements that were unknown and then the whole chain becomes unraveled. Over 40% of tested agricultural pesticides contain PFAS a forever chemical. It causes cancers of all kinds. Because they never go away, not from the environment not from our bodies. 99% of all humans have detectable levels of several PFAs. We are poisoning ourselves. (Ref: Biology news, By Kelk School of Medicine USC, Apr 2023)

Genetically Modified Food to Include Pesticides

Genetically modified food such as corn, soybeans, potatoes, have been genetically engineered. Corn as an example has been changed to be naturally insect resistant while tomatoes have been modified to slow down the rotting process. Farmers must get their seeds from these corporations to replant their crops. The final outcome and consequence of our intervention with the natural process is not fully understood but I damn well know the food does not taste as good as it did in the past. I do not appreciate eating GMO (Genetically Modified) corn that has (chemical) an insect resistant gene in it. It can cause allergic reactions and other health scares…It could be a contributing factor to antibiotic-resistance…It could be a carcinogen. How did we let this happen? (Ref: Insider GMO pros and cons)

"Let us permit nature to take her own way; she better understands her own affairs than we. Michael de Montaigne translated."

Agriculture

Agriculture, food and beverage touches every human on the planet refrigerated transportation, trucking and shipping products internationally around the world, to move the global economy requires a huge amount of energy and water to produce and move their products on a world scale.

Agriculture accounts for a significant amount of carbon production, besides the fuel required to power it. The Industrial agriculture model used to extract food from the ground needs

29

to change. We have turned farms into massive corporations that only turn out one type of crop, continuously year after year.

They use chemical fertilizers for the intensive agriculture; the chemicals cause the soils to die off. The nutrients are taken out of the soil and the artificial fertilizers used are not returning the nutrients to the soil. It reduces the future fertility of the soil and also causes huge amounts of carbon to be released from the soil into the atmosphere. The soil becomes a source for carbon emissions. The agriculture footprint on this planet must change; we do not want to get trapped by bureaucratic nonsense and industrialization of mass farming to the detriment of everything else. We must transform our agricultural processes. Farmers need to plant trees, stop using pesticide and or genetically modified seeds.

Why have farmers cut down the trees on their land? To maximize the growing space for crops; but it has had the opposite effect. We cut the trees to farm the land in order to farm more land and because there are no trees the soil loses its nutrients and the farms become less and less productive. The trees keep tons of water in the land; the trees provide the leaves that nurture the soil. The animals whose manure enriched the land are gone, because farmers now use tractors for efficiency. Running farms with fertilizers is only killing the soil. Soils are slowly turning into deserts the soil is dying, without rich soils you cannot hold the water, so it runs off the land with its fertilizers into the rivers.

When the rains come, there are no trees to hold the water and the land no longer holds the water and the fertilizers. Trees keep the water in the fields of the farms; they release oxygen in the air and fertilize the farmlands with their leaves, and remove co2 from the atmosphere. Trees provide shelter for birds and animals; they provide shade to all who sit under them. A healthy 100-foot-tall tree has about 200,000 leaves. A tree this size can hold **11,000 gallons** of water from the soil and release it into the air again, as oxygen and water vapor, in a single growing season. (Ref: Data Water and Forests)

Without change; protecting our bio diversity will not happen, soil needs organic matter from plants and animals not fertilizers. Agricultural farms are using 80 plus percent of the world's water, water is becoming more valuable than gold. (Ref: U.N. Food and Climate Change)

Soil

Soil is so important; we as a planet will find growing crops will become increasingly more difficult. This is our unconscious human behavior. We are causing massive erosion and desertification across the globe. Why is the earth's rich soil eroding to desertification? We are not adding organic content, the microbes necessary for rich soil nutrients. The soil then turns into sand when you remove the organic content. On a world scale, we are headed for a desertification that will destroy agriculture. The kind that was seen in North Africa thousands of years ago, we are repeating history, we never learn! Every country uses pesticides, herbicides, artificial fertilizers that are killing the soil. We are losing the biodiversity of the soil. Having removed the trees it exposes the soil to the sun and is getting hotter requiring more water of which there is less and less. Farm land must have different plants and trees to nurture the land. It is the cycle of life on the land and we ignore it to our own peril.

There will be deserts where there was once fertile land. Millions of creatures depend on a rich soil because very little life lives in a desert. The United Nations states the way we are presently farming we perhaps have only 50 years of farmable earth left. We are headed for soil extinction. Once there are no nutrients left in the soil of the earth, we will have forsaken this planet. It will become like the planet Mars. The World Economic Forum states in the next 30–50 years there will be a food crisis on the planet. We the intelligent creatures are on this path because we are unconscious of our actions. When the food crisis is upon us, the countries with the biggest armies will come and take the land and the food. There will be chaos, malnutrition, inhumanity everywhere. Not only the poor will die, the rich will also be the first to be killed by the poor. Remember Marie Antoinette.

Food, people are dying of hunger while the profiteers are making a killing on food. The UN says that 75 million people are malnourished because of the continuous rise in the price of foods.

"The earth and the soil are living entities. It is my wish and my blessing that we act as one humanity to turn the situation around from the brink of disaster. Save soil. Let us make it happen." – Sadhguru

Plastics

There are many environmental issues that must be addressed like plastics. Globally to date, there are about **8.3 billion tons** of plastics in the world—some 6.3 billion tons of that is trash. The majority of plastics are single use disposable (that is a word that should be outlawed 'Disposable') that will go to the garbage dump within a year, where they will persist for centuries, finally ending in the oceans polluting the environment. People are exposed to chemicals from plastic multiple times per day through the air, dust, water, food and use of consumer products. Phthalates are used as plasticizers in the manufacture of vinyl flooring, wall covering, food packaging, and medical devices. Eight out of every ten babies and nearly all adults have measurable levels of phthalates in their bodies. We are slowly poisoning ourselves and the environment. There are many future consequences that remain unchallenged, such as cardiovascular diseases, age and puberty, obesity, and developmental disorders yet to raise their ugly heads on our medical futures. (Data, Phthalates The Everywhere Chemical).

Micro plastics, are produced when synthetic clothes break down into smaller fibers, think every time we wash clothes nano plastics is washed into our rivers and oceans. Polluting our oceans with microscopic shards of plastic polymers. It has been scientifically found (Science alert.com) nano plastics latch on to neural crest cells causing deformation in embryos. Micro plastics come from these common fabrics, polyesters, nylons, acrylics, spandex, fleece. Every time we wash these clothes, and they release microplastics in the environment to be consumed by animals and then in turn get consumed by humans.

Oh, the insanity!

Scientists have discovered a new disease called 'Plasticosis' in Seabirds that have ingested plastics. Over 90% of Seabirds have ingested plastics. (Ref: The Guardian New disease caused by plastics). The seabirds will die.

There is plastic floating the oceans as far as the North and South Poles, and sinking to the ocean as white specs of plastic that fish mistake as plankton, and eat the plastics and die. Plastic bags, bottle tops, foam cups and all sorts of plastics are found in stomachs of dead sea lions, dolphins, sea turtles. British Scientists discovered that microscopic pieces of plastic can be found everywhere in the oceans, even inside plankton, the keystone of the marine food chain. (Ref: Nature—Plastic pollution in the arctic)

The great Pacific Garbage Patch (Island of plastics refuse floating in the Pacific Ocean) is 1.6 million square kilometers twice the size of Texas, three times the size of France (Ref: Ocean Cleanup .com)

Oh, the insanity of humanity. Plastic when it breaks down mimic's plankton. Plankton is the very base of the food chain, we destroy this base, and we destroy every living creature in the ocean. The health of the oceans is intimately connected to human health. We are killing the ocean that supports us all.

We cannot let this continue. The insanity.

Humans have covered the entire planet with plastic debris, we have cause irreversible damage to all life on this planet. Oh, the Insanity.

"The human race will be the cancer of the planet." Julian Huxley, attributed.

Plastics will be the final nail in the coffin for all life in the ocean. We need laws to be changed and enforced to prevent plastics being made or discarded in land fill. Marine wildlife is eating plastic because it looks like plankton. Then humans eat the fish this will cause many unknown illnesses, and even death to ourselves.

"The packaging for a microwave dinner is programmed for a shelf life of maybe six months, a cook time of two minutes and a landfill dead-time of centuries" – David Wann, Buzzworm Nov 1990.

The natives only took what they needed. Now we need to protect whatever species are left. There used to be

35

millions of buffaloes roaming the western prairies fertilizing the fields. The natives only took what they needed. The west was ideal land to farm, now no longer, with all the chemicals and pesticides being used on farms it is destroying the productivity of the land itself.

"When we Indians kill meat, we eat it all up...when we build houses, we make little holes. When we burn grass for grasshoppers, we don't ruin things. We shake down acorns and pine nuts. We don't chop down the trees"—Wintu Indian, quoted in Julian Burger, The Gaia Atlas of First Peoples 1990.

Fish

By mid-century, there will be no fish in the ocean. Without fish we have no functioning eco system in the ocean. Without a functioning ocean we do not have a functioning atmosphere. Without a functioning atmosphere we are all literally living in misery. Without the life in the oceans we will die. 70 billion people on the planet catching the very last fish, over fishing, trawling, long lines have decimated the fish population. 40 to 50 billion fish species have been killed fishing for prize fish like shrimp, tuna and cod, halibut, 90% thrown back and die, now they do not throw the unwanted fish back they keep them to feed pigs! Have we all gone mad? China is out roaming the seas to find food for its population of 1.45 billion people. (data Fish and overfishing)

"It is curious situation that the sea from which life first arose should now be threatened by the activities of one form of that life." – Rachel Carson

Overfishing; when we buy a fish in the market, we do not realize the harm that has been used in order to obtain that fish, prawn, tuna etc. We over fish till there are basically none left. Why would we do that? In the beginning we caught fish as we needed, now, we catch fish indiscriminately that is the big fish and we are fishing the big fish into extinction. To get the big fish like Halibut, cod, tuna and other prize fish we cast huge nets that trawl the oceans and pick up all manners of creatures. These creatures support every other creature within the oceans; we are causing a massive ocean extinction of species we have not even yet scientifically identified. At first, we threw back the fish we did not need, of which more than 80%–90% had already died. Now, we keep them and feed them to pigs, while the life within the oceans is dying in front of our eyes. We are emptying the oceans of sea life, is this not insane? We use huge nets, and huge ships that can catch and process fish right on the ocean. Trawlers troll the bottom of sea and oceans to pick up prawns. These nets destroy the plants and the and the creatures that live on the bottom of the seas and oceans that are required to support the life around them. If you wanted to catch a rabbit, would you cast a net over the whole town and catch many other things only to throw them away except for the rabbit? This is what trawlers with huge nets in the ocean actually do. About 95% of marine life caught by a typical shrimp trawler dies on deck and is discarded. The global fishing fleet, of modern industrial fleet has turned our seas and oceans into a vast killing field that is unsustainable. Why should this concern us? Three times the number of other sea creatures (by weight) died in the process of catching the prized fishes. Much of the by catch is made up of rare and slow growing species which will take decades to recover if ever. This is a calamity, but like climate catastrophe ignorance is no longer palatable. (Ref: Greenpeace Fish don't stand a chance—Author Unknown)

Only our intelligence without consciousness would allow this to happen.

Large parts of nets or lines are lost at sea or in the ocean. These lines and nets entangle all manner of wild life from birds, to whales, to fish that get entangled and cannot escape, as this massive killing floats in the open waters. Humanity is insane.

"Fishing with modern technology is the most destructive activity on earth and modern technology is the most destructive activity on earth." – Charles Clover (Environment Correspondent Daily Telegraph.)

The Fish are massacred in the billions die and then we wonder what happened to all the billions of tons of fish that the oceans used to produce. We over fish and poison the oceans we poison ourselves.

We are so intelligent we fish only those species that are valuable to sell and throw back all other species that have died before they can be returned. We disrupt nature's life cycle and bounty. We fish the oceans endlessly. We are destroying the very environment in which fish need to survive by taking the very food they need to survive. Even the animals like the lion will not kill all of its preys only to have nothing left. Yet, that is exactly what we are doing to all of nature.

Tunas used to be plentiful in the ocean, they used to weigh hundreds of pounds, now they are small yet we continue to fish them to hunt for the last one. It takes 3 to 5 years for a tuna to reach sexual maturity, yet we catch them before then. Fish is not a commodity, yet we are fishing the last Tuna for $275,000 dollars (Ref: Yahoo Finance/ Robb Report), complete insanity. Being so rare it brings a terrible absurdity as they are hunted even more to extinction. What a fallacy in human behavior. It is a calamity that a rare fish becomes so valuable. People become relentless to catch them. Can we not see? Are we that blind? There is only one outcome it can only be very bad, a planet with no fish at all. The economies of things that are rare become even more valuable for humanity to capture and kill. I ask are we insane?

Are we going to keep catching all the fish till there are no more? Are we that insane? All fish life has been depleted by 90% yet we continue fishing no one is policing the oceans! We are stripping the oceans of life and not replacing it. (Data fishing and overfishing).

Dams

The cross-border fight for water by Jean Philippe Chognot. "Ethopian megadam on the Nile is subject of a regional dispute with Egypt and Sudan. The Dam in Turkey sucks water out of two great rivers the Tigres and Euphrates. Iraq and Syria say Turkey's dam resulted in a reduction of water flowing in their lands. The Itiapo dam on the Parana river is a source of tension between Brazil and Paraguay. China's Mekong Dam feeds more than 60 million people through its basin and tributaries to Thailand, Laos, Myanmar, Cambodia and Vietnam. The Kashmir dam on the Indus river between India and Pakistan.

Huge dams are constructed to preserve water and create electricity while neighbors go dry causing world conflicts."

Rivers are the source of life. In temperate climates (warm climates) in the past 20 to 25 years, the reservoirs are depleted, the rivers are being depleted; they are less than

50% of what they were. We are trying to hold waters in reservoirs, look how well that has worked in California, now there is no water for the rivers, many years of drought, the soil, the trees, the wetlands, they are the source for holding water. Rivers are drying before reaching the oceans, the oceans enter the rivers as salt water, the lands along the rivers will be arid and brown, and they will be lost. Dams are empty till the rains come then they are filled to the brim you cannot hold back the water which is released and causes floods in the towns downstream because we have cut the trees that hold the water. Farmers will struggle to produce food, going from heat where there is not enough water to having floods and too much water destroying their crops.

Why should I care? As time marches on each generation forgets the bounty of this planet as our intelligence thinks we can out think nature. There used to be millions upon millions of salmon swimming upstream to spawn. The natives said there was so many you could cross the river on their backs. No more. We, in our intelligence, built dams to produce electricity, to store and divert water to farms, and the salmon can no longer swim upstream to spawn.

I could go on and on but our own intelligence has turned against us, what intelligent creature would hunt his food till there is none left? We are so intelligent we put a monetary value on trees, plants and animals and fish on a higher plane than life itself. (Data Environmental impacts of Dams)

"We abuse the land because we regard it as a commodity belonging to us. When we see land as a community to which we belong, we may begin to use it with

love and respect." – Aldo Leopold, A Sand county Almanac.

Remember

"Suburbia is where the developer bulldozes out the trees, and then names the streets after them." – Bill Vaughn.

Remember as a child you could go to the countryside and if there was a stream you could drink from that stream. I use to drink the water that ran down the rivers and now I cannot even swim in them. No more. Remember when you could swim in the ponds and rivers. No More. Remember when you could swim in the ocean near the city. No more. I use to fish in the lakes and streams to eat the fish, no more because they are poisoned with our pollution. Is this right? What is wrong? Remember when you could eat the snow as it fell from the sky. No more. Remember when you used to climb the old tree in the yard, no more, because it has been cut down. Remember when a tomato tasted like a tomato, you could eat it like an apple it was so good. No more. Remember when the air was so fresh, full of oxygen from the trees. No more. Then we ask why did we cut the trees?

Remember when the soil was so fertile you could grow anything. No more. Why, because it is no longer fertile, there are no animals to fertilize the fields and there are not any leaves from trees to turn to compost.

Remember we could drink water from the wells in our back yard. No more. Where there is gas exploration, they put poisonous chemicals into the ground and these chemicals flow with the water into wells poisoning the water.

Remember when Captain Cook discovered the Hawaiian Islands? Were the natives working or were they enjoying life? They did not catch all the fish, they were smart they closed their bay to the fish and only caught the fish they needed from the bay. They left the rest to continue to breed and multiply they never ran out of fish. Oh, by the way they did not work they enjoyed life.

Climate Catastrophe

Global warming does not affect me, why should I care? As we continue to pump more carbon dioxide, from the Billions of gasoline cars, trucks, airplanes, boats, we all drive every day. As long as we keep our economy growing our environments will keep dying...unless we change.

The billions of pounds of carbon dioxide from coal fueled electricity, the billions of tons of natural gas that fuels industry. Oil well and gas wells spew methane in the search for gas and oil. There is also naturally occurring methane from agriculture, swamps, decaying plants.

The oil industry continues to deny that global warming even exists. We continue to drive our cars; we continue to burn coal for electricity, we continue to use gas. We must keep the economy going. The economy is killing us!!!!

What is the definition of insanity to continue to do the same thing and expect a different outcome?

What will be the outcome of a continuous global warming? Oceans act as a massive sponge, soaking up more than a quarter of the CO_2 humans pump into the atmosphere. When this sponge becomes too saturated, it warms the oceans and kills marine life, and disrupts the delicate balance of the ecosystem that all life on earth depends. All of sudden weather patterns become very unpredictable, countries have no rain for years, fires break out everywhere and we are just at the tip of cataclysmic planetary behavior. We are creating a climate time bomb.

Global warming affects everyone on this planet. We have seen it where it would normally rain it has suddenly been re-categorized as an atmospheric river, a description as of the size of 15 Mississippi Rivers are unleashed from the skies. All low land areas near rivers and waterways will be flooded. As the ocean raises from the higher temperatures all countries below sea level will be flooded. Think of Bangladesh, islands around the world, Vienna, Vancouver, New York, Hawaii, all the lower land in and around oceans, seas will not be safe the lower basin of Vancouver have already been flooded, Sumas in Washington State, areas of New York under water the list goes on and on. This is during the rainy season; we feel the effects of the heat in the summer. Can you not see the correlation of it all? The hot scorching summer heat of California's burning sun. Europe is burning, British Columbia is burning. There will be intolerable heat in the desserts of California, Africa and Saudi Arabia.

Global warming will cause a mass migration and displacement of humanity the likes of which has never been seen. Humanitarian organizations will not be able to respond, millions will die, and there will be a massive civil unrest and chaos in many nations. Humanity will not know how to respond to empty food shelves.

"Humanity is on the march, earth itself is left behind."
– David Ehrenfeld, The arrogance of Humanism, 1978.

We are all asleep at the switch, afraid to push the stop insanity button. I do not want to get technical, because technicalities put people to sleep.

As greenhouse gas emissions heat the planet further, the ecological and climate systems that humans have relied on for millennia is unraveling, a sort of chain reaction that will continue to have stronger and stronger impacts of climate catastrophe exponentially.

3 degrees Celsius change may not seem like a shocking number. We think it is just a trivial number. It has massive far-reaching implications that unbalance what nature has created very slowly to a massive change and dire consequence for all humanity.

We just keep getting warmer we have all seen it. In our lifetimes, we are experiencing the worst conditions on this planet. It keeps getting hotter and hotter yet we are in denial. Texas is on fire yet we continue to deny.

The past decade was the hottest in recorded history, and this decade is on pace to break that record. Heat waves and higher temperatures will cause premature deaths to millions.

The fossil fuel industry continues to be subsidized by our tax dollars even as forests burn, the ocean heats up, the poles melts, and animals all over the world lose their habitat. Most of the world's coastal cities will face substantial flooding, and storms. The ocean is absorbing the majority of the excess heat trapped in the atmosphere by greenhouse gases and, as it heats, weather patterns will become more unpredictable.

Climate catastrophe is changing weather patterns, creating unprecedented downpours, droughts and floods. Both drought and floods can destroy agriculture, displace people from their homes, and wipe out economies.

Extreme rainfall will cause floods and then droughts which will fuel forest fires and cause desertification.

Climate catastrophe will cause a further wildlife extinction, animal and plant kingdoms will be wiped out as temperatures rise and the hotter it gets, their habitats the forests they live in get destroyed by human activity. The oceans will become warmer killing corals and fish that cannot live in warmer waters.

Tropical storms have been getting stronger, faster, and more destructive due to warming ocean temperatures, rising sea levels, and other planetary shifts. Under all warming scenarios, category 4 and 5 tropical storms would become a more frequent event. We have seen it yet we continue to deny it.

Climate catastrophe will kill far more people than the COVID-19 pandemic through heat waves, waterborne illnesses, air pollution, and much more. Yet we stay inactive.

The World Health Organization warns that drought is expected to displace 700 million people by 2030 alone. Climate catastrophe will cause the world's biggest humanitarian and refugee crisis we have witnessed. (U.N. Report "Now or Never" to avoid climate catastrophe, Apr 2022)

This is the fall of Rome, when the Romans could not stop the barbarians from wanting the riches of Rome. The barbarians will be upon the civilized world unless we change, and like the Romans we will not be able to stop them. Think of the Aztecs, the Mayans, the Egyptians, civilizations don't last forever. The current civilization is far more complex involving all the countries of the world. No one sees that we are all interconnected and our drive for uncontained economic growth is suffocating this planet. The unbridled economic activities tied to profits will result in the demise of this planet.

They will come by the billions. We see this in Europe and that is just from religious and political causes. Whole country evacuations and migrations have not begun to unravel yet, but it will. Millions and billions will be displaced causing pain and anguish yet we are in denial.

The planet is rebelling against humanity, we are the virus, think COVID—it is only the start. Think no food no job on a dead planet! The planet who has been here for billions of years will decide our future. It will continue to make life miserable for all humanity. We are disconnected from the very planet we all live on. We are unconscious of the beauty and magnificent of the nature around us that supports our lives. We must take our consciousness to a new level not to rape the planet for profit but to enhance all life and the lives of every human that inhabit this planet. We must enhance our lives and to do this we must nourish and protect the planet. All people are looking for better lives, but we must take care of all the living things on this planet. We are not doing that we are destroying the very planet that gave rise to our human intelligence or, should I say human insanity?

"I would feel more optimistic about a bright future for man if he spent less time proving that he can outwit nature and more time tasting her sweetness and respecting her seniority." – Elwyn Brooks White. Essays of E.B. White 1977.

The biggest mistake the world is making is to believe the oil, coal, gas, automotive, and chemical industries.

How do we stop? We do not fix the problem we address the symptoms. The forest fires rage on and we use water and chemical retardants to stop the fires. The root cause of global warming is not being addressed properly. We cannot wait 20 or 30 years or 50 years as conditions continue to worsen. We will no longer be here in 200 years if we continue.

Civilization as we know it is on a point of no return, we may not last into the next century.

Nuclear Waste

Why would an intelligent species want to commit genocide of each other willingly? What intelligent species would want to destroy the planet that over billions of years, developed into a garden of Eden. I ask Why????

Plutonium can remain radioactive for thousands of years. (Ref: Radioactive Waste/EPA.)

Here are the countries that have nuclear bombs and the number of tests each country has exploded the bomb into the atmosphere or other.

Countries that have atomic bombs—N. Korea, Iran, USA, Israel, China, Pakistan, India, France, Russia, England, South Africa, Ukraine, Kazakhstan.

The number of nuclear tests by country, USA-1,032; Russia-727; UK-88, France 217, China-47, India-3, Pakistan-2, N Korea-6.

Where does all this nuclear waste go? Foreign governments are so secretive, they will not tell their population where they have buried the nuclear waste. For the USA it is much easier to list the states that do not have nuclear waste. MT, ND, WY, SD, AK, HI, NM, OK, KY, WV, DE, RI.

Data from Maxx Chatsko 2019.

How much nuclear waste does your state hold? Where is it stored?

This is a very sad story that turned an island paradise to a hell of atomic tests, the Marshall Islands. The Marshall Islands is a disaster in the making. The USA from 1946 to 1958 did nuclear tests across the islands.

The radioactive waste is stored in a concrete tomb on Rundit Island. 3.1 million cu. Ft. of nuclear waste is contained within. The US also shipped an additional 130 tons of radioactive waste from Nevada. Plutonium 23 takes 24,000 years to reach a half-life.

Sea water has been seeping into the tomb from the Pacific Ocean. It is a decade old decaying structure, polluting pristine waters. The ocean level is rising with global warming and will submerge the island as well as the nuclear tomb. The collapse of tomb's dome will release all the nuclear contaminates into the Pacific Ocean. Thousands of dead fish wash up on the shore as of this writing. It is one of the 21st century greatest nuclear disaster. Much of the Marshall Islands are uninhabitable, worse than the Chernobyl disaster. "Out of sight out of mind" Oh the human insanity. (Ref: How the US betrayed the Marshall Islands—Los Angeles Times, Susan Rust.)

Meat

Think of all the beef that is required to serve the billions of hamburgers, and all those animals emit methane gases.

Philip Wollen is an Australian philanthropist, environmentalist and animal rights activist. (Below is his Speech on Animal rights).

"Animals must be off the menu they are screaming in terror. In slaughterhouses in crates and in cages and when they suffer, we suffer as equals. Meat is more murderous than tobacco. CO_2 methane and nitrous oxide from the livestock industry are killing our oceans with acidic hypoxic dead zones. We are depleting the oceans as 90 % of small fish are ground up into pellets to feed livestock. Vegetarian cows today are the world's largest ocean predators. The oceans are the lungs and the arteries of the earth, yet the oceans are dying, by 2050 all our fisheries will be depleted. Millions of bouncy little chicks are ground up alive simply because they are male to feed cattle that are vegetarians. Only 100 billion people have ever lived, 7 billion people live today and yet we torture and kill 2 billion living creatures every week. 10, 000 entire species are wiped out every year because of the actions of one species—humanity! We are now facing the 6th mass extinction in cosmological history. If any other organism did this, a biologist would call them a virus. It is a crime against (humanity) of unimaginable proportions.

"The human race will be the cancer of the planet," – Julian Huxley attributed.

Animal rights are now the greatest social justice issue since the abolition of slavery. There are 600 million vegetarians in this world, yet we are still drowned out by the raucous hunting, shooting, killing cartels that believe that violence is the answer when it should not even be a question. Meat kills animals, kills us and is killing our planet. Cornell and Harvard say that the optimum amount of meat in a healthy human diet is zero. Water is the new oil. Nations will soon be going to war for it. Underground aquifers that took millions of years to fill are now running dry. It takes about 1500 liters of water to produce 1 kilogram of wheat, and it takes an astounding **10 times more** to produce the same amount of beef. Today 1 billion people are hungry, 20 million people will die from malnutrition. Cutting meat by only 10% will feed 100 million people. And eliminating meat will end starvation. If everyone ate a western diet, we would need two planets to feed us and we only got one and she is dying. Live stocks generate roughly 15% of Global Greenhouse gas emissions compared to 25% in transportation. Poor countries sell grain to the west while their own children starve in their arms. And the west feed it to livestock so we can eat a steak. Am I the only one who sees this as a crime? Every slice of meat we eat is slapping a tear-stained face of a starving child. When I look into her eyes, do I remain silent?

The earth can produce enough food for everyone's need but not enough for everyone's greed. We are facing the perfect storm. But it's not a rogue state it's an industry it's every industry (The economic web) we can stop it. Our economic systems are the weapons of mass destruction.

The Stone Age didn't end because we ran out of stones this cruel disgusting industry will end because we run out of excuses.

Animals are just another species they are other nations. And we murder them at our peril; the peace map is drawn on a menu. Peace is not just the absence of war. It is the presence of Justice. Justice must be blind to race, color religion or species. If she is not blind, she will be a weapon of terror.

Another world is possible. And on a quiet night I can hear her breathing, let's get animals off the menu and out of the torture chambers. Talk for those that have no voice." PHILIP WOLLEN.

"Thank God men cannot fly, and lay waste the sky as well as the earth." – Henry David Thoreau.

Unfortunately we have, by putting satellites around the earth and then destroying them at life's end we have also created a trash that orbits around our planet, when will our stupidity and insanity stop? Can we not see, can we not open our eyes and say enough is enough! What happened to our consciousness of right and wrong?

Extinction

Our continued drive for better lives through increased economic growth is causing; as conservation experts have signaled, that the world is in the grips of a 'Sixth mass extinction' of species, driven by the destruction of natural habitat and climate catastrophe. *"If things aren't falling dead at your feet, that does not mean you are not in the middle of a big extinction event."* – Professor Norman Macleod: Paleontology, Natural Museum London.

Biologist E.O. Wilson once pondered whether many of our fellow living things were doomed once evolution gave rise to an intelligent, technological creature that happened to be insatiable and carnivorous, fiercely territorial and prone to very short-term thinking. We humanity has in essence triggered a 6th mass extinction one that will rival an asteroid impact like the one that killed most of the life on this planet. Species are going extinct all around us at an ever-increasing rate. A staggering number of amphibians, birds, insects, plants and wild animals are disappearing in front of our eyes. Yet, we do not see. We are pushing our ecosystems, the one that keep us alive beyond their breaking point. Additional atmospheric heat will cause more turbulence, and weather patterns will change in unpredictable ways, we pollute the air, the water, the ground, the rivers and oceans that change the atmosphere and cause extreme weather conditions. We have all seen it. If we do not take care of nature, nature will take care of us through powerful hurricanes, droughts, wild fires, rising oceans, burying complete countries that are below sea level, food shortages, famines and new diseases then wars and revolutions will develop until humanity is completely wiped out. Unless we change our collective consciousness, until all of humanity realizes we are all interconnected. Without worldwide cooperation we are on the verge of a total societal collapse. Or, we can change and reverse the destructive path we are on. We the people of this planet have the power to change directions and take the steps to consciously restore the planet's environment. We can consciously stop our insanity stop working for greed and live our lives every day helping one another.

"For 200 years we've been conquering nature. Now we are beating it 'to death." – Tom McMillan, quoted in Francesca Lyman, The Greenhouse Trap, 1990.

It is happening to us now and it is real.

It will take our planet 5 to 10 million years to recover its biodiversity, and it's never the same. Now, why should I be concerned if we are going to go extinct?

If someone came up to you one day and told you we are all living our lives **wrong** and we have to change our ways immediately or we (humanity) are all going to go extinct, what would you do?

That is the fundamental question, why should I even be interested? My life is fine I am working, earning money paying my rent or my mortgage, paying my loans making ends meet sometimes not, but on the whole manage to live in stress and anxiety sometimes wondering how we will get to next month.

We measure our success by our bank accounts, by our travels, by our possessions. Sometimes family and life take a back seat. We forget the simple things that used to be free like water, the quality of air the difference between clean air and city smog. You go to a forest and breath in the clean air that the trees and plants provide. You go to the city and you breathe in the smog from the carbon monoxide that cars produce. Do you not see? Yet we keep cutting down the forests to make more space for the city and farms. Can you not see? Can we knowingly allow our legacy as humanity to be the extinction of all other creatures by consumption, habitat destruction, exploitation for human commerce, pollution, disease. This is our legacy.

Am I Still Unconcerned???

Still do not see the correlation? Still do not see the dilemma that we are creating? Still do not see the future? There will be no future if we continue to be oblivious and unconscious to our own behaviors. Top scientists are already ringing the alarms but we are caught in inaction a stupor of 'cognitive impairment' we see it and yet as a global community we do nothing because we cannot stop the economy.

If we continue and do not change, we can expect a very terrible outcome for future generations. We have seen just the tip of the iceberg of our climate catastrophe; it is on our doorstep with the fires the floods.

"Our modern industrial economy takes a mountain covered with trees, lakes, running streams and transforms

it into a mountain of Junk, garbage, slime pits, and debris. "
– Edward Abbey.

"There are no nations there is only humanity. If we don't come to understand that right soon, there will be no nations because there will be no humanity." – Isaac Asimov.

Chapter 2
Economic Chains

What is the measure of success in life? People want to have a successful life style. Our idea of success is purely illusionary. It is not intelligence that we value, not wisdom that we value. Who is the most recognized person in America? People will only name the richest persons, actors and athletes. We will not know the wisest person, the educated person, the most scientific person, a religious man. People play sports and get paid well beyond what is reasonable to play a game. (Topic for another day) Why will people talk about the richest persons?

Then by default which is the richest nation? Power and money have become the highest goals which are a very tragic outcome when looking at our lives and does not allow us to embrace life and enjoy nature. Unknowingly the USA has taken on a leadership role in the world. In doing so, they have destroyed their environment yet the whole world wants to be like them. Does this make any sense? Really is that what we want? They can no longer drink the water from their rivers, the water of life. They destroy all of nature except for national parks, as the laws change even national parks are threatened by gas and oil exploration. Is that what we want? Americans put all types of various carbon dioxides in a bottle and drink it; a human body needs water and oxygen not carbon dioxide. Half the world drinks different kinds of carbonated water. To produce these carbonated beverages massive amounts of water is required. People do not know their planet but they know coca cola. How can that be? It is advertising, and marketing by big corporations. Big corporations rule our nation, not government.

"The richest nation does not translate to the richest culture, but does translate to a worsening environment of nature."

Every nation is striving to be affluent like the USA. Yet, we look around the globe many people are just struggling for survival, just to have one meal. This is senseless. Affluence means your survival needs have been met, but have they? People need three jobs just to survive and keep their heads above water. This is not an affluent society this is a tantamount to slavery. We must learn to sit back and enjoy life as it was given to us. The way we have structured civilization in the industrial age we cannot enjoy life. We are mortgaged to the bank; we have car loans, and have borrowed money for whatever reason. We must work for our lives, for what. You have made a 35 to 50-year economic commitment for your house mortgage.

"If Christ was to return and say follow me, you cannot, because you have financial obligations. When Christ was in Jerusalem 12 people followed, if he came back today how many would follow? You cannot change the direction of your life. If Christ says follow me, no one is going, we have monthly payments to take care of." – Sadhguru.

We have enslaved ourselves to our own financial chains. This is an insane way of organizing our lives and society. We work as slaves for forty fifty years and then we die, but have we enjoyed our life to the fullest. The very reason we want to become affluent is so we can change the direction of our lives whenever we want. Think about it! Being affluent should mean we should not be constantly battling for survival. Here we are an affluent society, but we need two to three jobs to survive. We are increasing our wants and needs (nice marketing word to develop needs we really don't need). We have 3 cars why? We are trying to be 'better than the Joneses'. We want our children to have more than what we had. This in turn drives us to have more and expect more. We are preached at every day to buy through daily ads there are more ads on TV than actual programming that is even worth listening to. Ads that tell us buy this you will be younger, you need this to make your life happier, a must have item for your home. These trigger inner desires to make your life better, but it only makes it worse. Your credit card debt is through the roof, it is out of control. How are you going to pay for everything? No matter what you do you are still fighting for survival. Have you noticed people who have less material things and work very little are actually happier people? Have you?

What do we want? If you have everything what do you want? I want a good paying job. What else do you want? I want to buy an apartment, a house. What else do you want? I want to buy a car. What else do you want? We need to work more. I need a vacation where I can enjoy and live a carefree life for two weeks. Work keeps us busy for forty or fifty years, searching jobs you hate to earn more income, so

I can buy more possessions. We work to the bone so much so we live to work. Let me repeat that we live to work. We work at two or three jobs a 16-hour work day for what? To buy things that will make my life easier. That much money, that much wealth it is always never enough. At the end, what does it all mean? Your death! Let it be known all these years you have worked and not enjoyed life at all. The material possessions you have accumulated you cannot take with you.

The fundamental question is do we need what we have compared to previous generations? Look at how much more we have, and the economic debt load we carry, that debt is also the debt (or should I say the toll) taken on nature. The debt of every household is the toll taken from nature. We need to cut our growth because we cannot continue to have all that we want. By consuming less, we are doing a great ecological service. Do we really need all that we have?

My X wife and I had a three-bedroom house (guests come once a year) completely furnished, a basement full of stuff, a garage full, two cars. I am also guilty of over consumption. When we are suddenly forced to downsize, because of family changes, health, or other issues, what happens? What happens to all that we got over the years and wouldn't let go? The kids come and take some, we sell or give away a lot, some to charity, yet there are two truckloads of stuff no one wants. Where does this go, landfill? We really only need what is necessary to live comfortably. When we die, no one wants it, and we cannot take it with us. All of us must adjust our lives; everyone in the world must live better and simpler lives of well-being. What is well-being, allow nature to flourish back to where it was when our ancestors were on this incredibly rich planet, with abundance everywhere. Everyone needs to cut down their possessions of what they own. It cannot be taken to their graves, but is carried on their backs as debt which forces us to be slaves to the economy. Doing work we hate because we must pay our debt.

The most important thing that is lost in the equation of economy is that we are alive, and our lives are tied to a vibrant planet that is also alive. But we are paying no attention to it as we continue on our march to destroy it. Trying to benefit ourselves, but when we destroy it, we unconsciously destroy ourselves.

We must cut down our expenses, limit our excesses, and work more in harmony with the planet not to the planet's detriment. We can take only what we need like our ancestors before us. We cannot continue to take without limit there will be nothing to take. To live and replace what we take is a simple process. We must bring our lives to some common sense. Our economic energy must be designed for the whole to the enhancement of all life on this planet. That is the key to the survival of humanity.

We humanity are like lemmings running headlong to the cliff, yet we know the cliff is there, we continue running, we are intelligent, so we run faster we have lost our consciousness. We see the cliff, we must stop, but we continue on the path that will lead to the destruction of future civilizations. We need to stop the relentless pursuit of economic wealth, stripping nature of everything, which is the cliff directly in front of us.

Think you are alive, your family is alive, your friends are alive, and that is the most precious thing. There is only one thing that is of immense value in your life and that is your life itself.

Did you live the happiest life in concert with nature or against it?

We lose sight of the big picture. Except for your work, your family, your ego nothing else is occurring. Your job is taking your life. Is your job fruitful; are you enhancing nature, or against nature. Is that what you want to do? Or, is it just to earn income to pay your bills, and buy more things. Ask the question what is guiding your life? Is this life yours, what you want, or are you in a raft letting the currents push you in whatever direction? Are you willfully directing the raft or are you just sitting in it letting life just happen?

What is your life, your career, your business, your family, are your yearnings going unfulfilled? If only I had this, if only I had those things, life would be so much better. If only I owned my own apartment. No! It is the things that you worked so hard to create that are taking your life. Can you not see?

We are unconscious of our own behaviors and the consequence of our behaviors. We need to question more of what is happening around us. That is why we ask questions. Children continually ask questions because they are curious, they still have a growing intelligence. Adults know the answers even if they do not know. We must look within ourselves are we even asking the question is full out economic growth the answer to resolve a disastrous growing debt by all nations? A question is a powerful tool. That question will take us to the next level of responsible consciousness on this planet. Can we not just admit that we in 200 years have committed the mistake of economic industrialization and start over? It is easy, we make the health of the planet the goal of any decision making. Can we not consciously as a species called humanity make an effort to start over by creating a new model for the entire planet to follow.

Human beings have a certain level of intelligence; this intelligence has led us to where we are. Now we need our consciousness to take over from our intelligence to get us to the next level. Get us past the ILLUSION of well-being through consumption. It is time to become responsible for all life on this planet. Survival is not the end game for humanity; survival has to be taken care of that is all. We this civilization everyone wants to live better than everyone else. This causes endless problems. In the economic growth competition that we are being driven to continuously improve, enhance, beautify, grow, upgrade, and on and on endlessly. We are trying to be better than everyone else. How much destruction we have caused and continue to cause to this planet is unimaginable, unbelievable. Yet we continue to destroy this planet which in turn will destroy us. We must stop the insanity!

Can we not see all the planetary disasters we have created through an unbridled economic growth policy? Humans are insensitive to all the life around us. We call this economic development. But we are really on a rampage of destruction and self-annihilation.

We must rethink our lives on this planet. We are all one we are all interconnected we all deserve to live life to the fullest working with and for the planet and only taking what is necessary for life. Our lives will be much more fulfilled when we work with nature and each other, rather than against nature and against each other.

"*Our complex global economy is built upon millions of small, private acts of psychological surrender, the willingness of people to acquiesce in playing their assigned parts as cogs in the great social machine that encompasses all other machines. The capacity for self-enslavement must be broken.*" – Theodore Roszak, The Voice of the Earth.

Chapter 3
How Did We Get Here
Economic Growth

Every day, governments report on the state of the economy; economy this, the economy that. all driven by unsustainable economic growth. Economic exploitation of natural resources on the backs of the population that work to buy and do not enjoy life. We are brained washed. A continuous and endless use of raw materials that is not endless. Whatever is produced packaged and shipped requires tons of energy which causes global warming. Then the stuff that is produced is returned to nature such as plastics, to pollute lifesaving water, kill the fish, the birds, and the fauna that we need to support the planet. We are not human beings we are slaves, unconscious of our condition. We cannot reduce global warming and emissions that cause global warming if we continue this pursuit of economic growth. If we continue growing the economy as we are, we will need more energy and materials.

3 years ago this report was published by CNN, and we as humanity occupying this planet have done nothing significant.

The occasion even has a name: Earth Overshoot Day. *"If Earth's resources were a bank account, today would mark the date we'd officially be in the red. As of July 29, humanity has officially used up more ecological resources this year than the Earth can regenerate by the end of the year."*

The Global Footprint Network, a sustainability organization which calculates the day, says humanity is currently consuming nature 1.75 times faster than the planet can regenerate.

That means we're overspending our natural capital, compromising resources in the future as a result and leading to things like deforestation and carbon dioxide buildup in the atmosphere.

And more carbon dioxide brings ever increasing climate catastrophe, the network says. It's getting worse.

A grim UN report The United States is one of the worst culprits.

If the entire world's population lived like Americans, the organization said, we would need five Earths to meet our demands. That's compared to countries like France or the United Kingdom, which would need less than three, which is suicidal. And, even though poorer countries aren't the ones overusing resources, they are the ones typically paying the costs. Research shows that climate catastrophe will more drastically affect poorer countries.

This data comes months after the United Nations released a landmark report, saying that humanity's pace of environmental destruction could endanger the 'ecological foundations of society'.

Continuing at the current pace, the report said, would create a global health emergency—potentially leading to millions of deaths from air pollution in Asia, the Middle East and Africa, and creating antimicrobial-resistant infections from freshwater pollution. By Leah Asmelash and Brian Ries, CNN Published, Mon July 29, 2019.

We have only got one Earth—this is the ultimately defining context for human existence.

Atomic energy, gas energy, oil energy, all producing toxic environmental gases producing greenhouse gases that will continue to produce unstable weather patterns, tidal floods, hurricanes and unseasonal weather patterns that will decrease the ability to grow food with regularity, it is a chain of events that humanity has caused through economic greed. Nuclear power may be considered a considered a cleaner energy, but radioactive substances spewed from the plants continue to contaminate areas and remain uninhabitable for thousands of years. If we cannot safely dispose of nuclear waste, we should look at another safer alternative energy.

"Environmentalist has long been fond of saying that the sun is the only safe nuclear reactor, situated as it is some 93 million miles away." – Stephanie Mills, In Praise of Nature, 1990.

Every government on the planet measures their economic success through GDP (Gross domestic product (GDP) it is the standard measure of the value added created through the production of goods and services in a country during a certain period. As such, it also measures the income earned from that production, or the total amount spent on final goods and services (less imports).

Our economic system is destroying our planet. We cannot reduce any kind of emission while carrying on an ever-growing economy. The more it grows, the more energy we need. All countries measure economic success in GDP. Yet, GDP does not account for the negative consequences of economic growth. It does not account for spewing CO_2 and methane; by extracting fossil fuels in the atmosphere and the planet heating up, it does not account for loss of wild life and fisheries, it does not account for soil erosion and flooding.

What makes sense today? Why are we continuing down this path of continued growth; increased GDP, increase exports, increase productivity, increase economic growth. Why are we continuing down this path even when we know that the outcome will not be good? The planet cannot sustain continued economic growth for 8 billion people. It is a physical insanity. Economy is not the solution to all our financial problems. What was a possibility 100 years ago is no longer relevant. The Cultural Revolution, the industrial revolution, we must change our economic model. We need to take a step back to a simpler time of joy and wonderment to what was the bounty that nature offered us. We need to open up a new possibility with nature itself. That is more sensible and sustainable than what we are doing now.

We have a limited planet with a limited amount of resources with a limited amount of water with an ever-increasing population going after more and more limited resources of land, water, and wildlife. This is a recipe for disaster.

We continue to want to improve living conveniences for humanity to the destruction of everything else around us. Our own intelligence has turned against us. We are consuming more than what is necessary to live.

We must control our human aspiration for more material things. We must if the planet is to have more children we must live within our desires on a healthy planet. Everyone wants to live the lifestyle of a US citizen, always consuming more. It will be a shame if we stand by on this planet and do nothing either to curb excess consumption or excess births, if we continue on this path there will be nothing left to consume.

We must consciously develop a culture of health; we must create a healthy society. We are living and behaving like cavemen. All societies are heading the way of the USA, always wanting more to become affluent, to have cars and more and more material things to carry on their backs. Where do these material things come from? Ask yourself, open your eyes!

Capitalism has given free rein to corporations to destroy our environment for the profit of their own pockets. The agenda of fossil fuel corporations is in itself malicious in the pollution of the earth's atmosphere and profiting from the destruction of life on earth. Well-funded organizations continue to claim climate denial which is upon us. This is a crime against humanity and should be prosecuted.

There are people that close a blind eye seeing their own planet being destroyed, the people that profit from an ever-increasing economic activity from the growth and sales of every conceivable product. We must re-think the well-being of the planet before the profits of the few.

We have what I call developed a **'Web of entanglement'.**

All humans want in their lives is conveniences. Look at all the people that have well-paying jobs, miserable people that are unhappy and unfulfilled. They have high blood pressure and the debt is so high they have to work more. They have all kinds of ailments anxiety and pressures. What do we want? We keep fooling ourselves in every step of our lives, by wanting more material things and then we prepare for your funeral. Have you lived your life, or is life passing you by?

We are so consumed by our own lives we do not see the big picture. We are consumed by an ever-increasing fuel to buy and spend. We are engulfed in continuous advertisements to buy more and more consumer goods to fuel an ever-growing economy. America and the world are about the pursuit of material things. It has morphed into the idea that this is happiness. It is not. People's memories are very short and corporations have overly capitalized on this. The dominant message found in all corporate messages links our most basic needs, and worse, the needs of our babies to consumer things and forcing all our energies into consumerism. Consumerism is what keeps corporations alive. It is estimated that the average American sees more than 32,000 TV commercials every year that is more than 320,000 by the time you become ten years old. You have been converted into a 'Buy Junkie'. American Corporations spend more than $110 billion on advertising every year. We have created a subliminal new religion, and we are unconscious to its consequences. 67 million cars produced last year pumping $co2$ in the atmosphere, 1.5 billion cell phones sold each year, 25 trillion tons of consumerism garbage heading to landfills. Unethical marketing managers, misleading advertising, deceptive promotions, false promises, fine print, TV ads and any other method is used to sell the consumer. It is working there is over consumption and huge waste in one half the world and we are told we need more. These marketing machines have influenced our world in the wrong way. Does anybody care?

One of the most positive things we can do for ourselves is to turn off the TV and give our tired receptive mind a complete break from the non-stop rush of information, misinformation and mindless entertainment that manipulates our fears and turns us into vegetables. Go outside enjoy whatever nature we have left, go and socialize with your neighbors, be alive. (Ref: Data Consumerism and the effects on climate change. Ref: Consumerism the world's fastest growing religion. C. Lasch.)

"Today's worst addictions are not marijuana, cocaine or even alcohol. They are the addictions to money and self, and in the relentless pursuit of self-satisfaction, it is often the children who are the casualties." – Frank Jones.

While we do this, no one is looking at the impact that it is having on the planet and it's interconnectivity to our basic lives. We continue to live an ever-stressful life chasing money and material things at an ever-increasing pace. We never actually get to the next plateau in our lives. Being unhappy, unfulfilled and always wanting more and getting less. We pursue wealth to apply the American dream of having it all to the detriment of everything else. This by definition drives people to insane measures by extracting everything that nature gives us. We are not living in sync with nature but against it. We must replenish what we take.

Somewhere I read we are hunting trees the way we hunted buffaloes are we also going to wipe out the trees, will we wipe out the Amazon?

"So bleak is this picture…that the bulldozer and not the atomic bomb may turn out to be the most destructive invention of the 20th century." – Philip Shabecoff, New York Times Magazine, 4 June 1978.

We cannot continue down the path of consumerism with no regards to the limit of nature. Nature can provide for all, but not when a ravenous creature like humans, take and take and take and give back very little. Evolution has created a species with intelligence yet we do not use this intelligence to live in harmony with nature, we use it to rape the planet's bounty to our own peril. World population is a serious problem. It is a constraint that all nations will need to accept a limitation on population growth. This in itself will be a huge problem unrestrained growth in population and consumerism is a recipe for a disaster. We can consume less voluntarily.

"Nature provides a free lunch, but only if we control our appetites." – William Ruckelshaus, Business Week, 18 Jun 1990.

We have a limited planet with a limited amount of resources with a limited amount of water with an ever-increasing population going after more and more limited resources of land, water, and wildlife. This is a recipe for disaster.

"Man will survive as a species for one reason: He can adapt to the destructive effects of our power-intoxicated technology and of our ungoverned population growth, to the dirt pollution and noise of New York or Tokyo. And that is a

tragedy. It is not man the ecological crisis threatens to destroy but the quality of human life." – Rene Dubois quoted in Life 28 July 1970.

There will be no quality of life.

Chapter 4
We Must Disentangle the 'Economic Web'

What is the "Web of Entanglement"? It is a web mankind has created and we cannot get out of this entanglement. It starts with the economy, which is taken from nature and requires massive amounts of energy and power to drive. The economy produces a false sense of wealth and employment that produces taxation. The taxation pays for industries that drive the economy and employment. The US debt in August 2020 was 26.7 trillion dollars. What is the US economic debt now? As of February 2022, the total debt was 30.29 trillion dollars and is ever increasing. All countries operate with a debt some much more than others, unfortunately we have tied economic growth to pay down the debt. Can you not see the fallacy of this policy, it is going to fail. The Planet is going to fail, and we are the cause.

We cannot sustain an economy that will never pay off this debt. All countries have tied their economy to pay off their debt. It will never happen. It is insanity, but yet we continue as if it is written in stone and cannot be changed. And the corporations that continue to rape and pillage nature have politicians in their back pocket so that laws favor the corporation and not the lives of the ordinary citizen which is being robbed of nature every day. We are all in this web of entanglement with no government exit strategy.

Politicians make laws, politicians are elected by the people to make laws that are supposed to benefit the people, and we have created great criminal laws. Where the government falls seriously short is in protecting the people's environment. Where we fall drastically short is in our environmental laws, particularly a World Environment Law, and a strong military force to enforce those laws. Unfortunately, politicians are funded by corporations that pass laws that favor those corporations. Corporations are chasing profits, and have little regard for the environment. Corporations have politicians on their board of directors to protect their own interests. They have lobbyists and lawyers to protect their interests.

Ordinary people buy stocks in corporations funding their resources hoping these corporations do well to obtain monetary compensation, are they going to speak out against these corporations. No! People drive cars every day, everyone contributes to global warming because they are chasing jobs that destroy the environment. We ourselves are the enemy.

The system needs to come crashing down! We need to say, continued unbridled economic growth was a good idea that has led us to where we are today. We need to start over with a clean slate. The health of the planet must come first.

"For 200 years, we've been conquering nature. Now we are beating It to death." – Tom McMillan, quoted in Francesca Lyman, The Greenhouse Trap. 1990.

Chapter 5
Unconscious Behavior

We lead lives without consciousness. You got your job perhaps by chance, now you may be stuck doing something you do not like. Why? The dollars are right, but your life is wrong. This leads to stress, ulcers health issues yet we continue to march on. We get married, subconsciously it is the right person, but 20 years later it is not. We all think we made a conscious choice. But was it? In life we are what we choose. And we do it without full consciousness. We lead our lives unconsciously, we all do it. We are not conscious of our selfishness. Ego kills consciousness. We are not looking at life sensibly.

How conscious are we as human beings? Why are people not conscious? We have gotten trapped into our daily lives, driven by survival and an ever-growing ego and materialism that feed this ego. We have ourselves become too egoistic, and are focused on improving me myself, and I. Until this limitation is overcome, we cannot realistically achieve consciousness. We are caught in the wave of societal influences, norms and beliefs. Ads and marketing, all influencing us to buy more, to get more which only leads to more destruction of nature. We are blind, a non-recognition of our destruction of nature, wild life and ourselves. As we continue on this path there is no way to be conscious of what we do around us. It becomes self-defeating; the whole world is not naturally enlightened, because we are too consumed about our own lives.

Do not worry about ecological issues, everything is fine let us keep doing what we have been doing for the last 200 years. It is not fine. We are blind; we do not see what is right in front of our eyes. Whenever humans think something is right why change it. As we learn over time what is right today is not necessarily right for tomorrow. We are unconscious to the very destruction that is occurring because of human behavior. We do everything that only matters to us, and we are keeping God as our final insurance policy. Our education, our memories our upbringing our beliefs has skewed our lives. Advertisements and the internet have filled our minds with false information. Companies and corporations manipulate our thoughts on what is right and what is wrong. We know what is right, we see what is wrong and we have the power to change our lives.

When are we going to figure out that our own well-being is not dictated by things but rather by human connection to each other and the planet we live on? When?

Most human beings take themselves too seriously, we do not understand we are all part of the puzzle, we either work with nature and the planet or the planet will work against us. We are a life on the planet like any other life, one second in universal time that is what you are in the cosmos of the universe. Yet, we feel so important. This is our heaven or our hell; it is for us to choose. We need to learn how to live well on this planet here and now but we must live in conjunction with the planet not against it. All the fools who think they are rich who have raped this planet, they have made a mess of this place. The problem is everyone is like this, everyone does it are we all insane? Oh, the insanity.

We are totally unconscious of what we do. Must we kill every gnat and pest that flies into our yard? Who is to decide what is a weed, and what is not? How did grass become a favored weed? Why do we put destructive pesticides on our lawns to keep it green, why does it need to be green? Why do we water it, only to drive the pesticides into our streams and rivers killing and poisoning fish? Why must it be a lawn? Why can we not have a front yard full of flowers so bees can enjoy them.

"The insufferable arrogance of human beings to think nature was made solely for their benefit" Savinien de Cyrano de Bergerac, Etats et empires de la lune 1656.

We wipe out species after species, where have all the birds gone? It is said that 200 species disappear from the planet every day. How could we let this happen?

The elephants are one of the most intelligent and passionate animals on the planet, yet we continue to hunt them mercilessly for their ivory tusks. Are we insane?

We have a right to take a life be it a plant or animal to nourish ourselves, but we have no right to take as many animals as possible for profit or pleasure. We have no right to put a dollar value on animal, plant, a tree. We have become a scourge a parasite on this planet. In an asylum only, the doctors look crazy. When are we going to come to the realization that we cannot continue down this path of unconsciousness.

Human beings are adaptable, we will adapt to very hot or very cold temperatures and an increasingly worse planetary conditions more storms, more tornados much stronger hurricanes, high seas and oceans coastal flooding, river swelling and flooding. Why? Why do we need to adapt when we can easily change our interaction with the planet? We can change to have a better life by being intelligent creatures on this planet and enjoy its fruit and bounty before it is all gone. We need to stop destroying and plundering it incessantly. It is our choice, if we do not make the right choice, we will be a virus this eco system will eventually exterminate. *"Whoever opens their eyes there is light to see."* The planet does not discriminate between an insect and a human being. The planet treats everyone and everything the same way. The sun is in the sky for all, life on this planet is inclusive, wherein there is no discrimination. That is the truth; the untruth is destroying life to benefit who?

"Every creature is better alive than dead, men and moose and pine trees, and he who understands it will rather preserve its life than destroy it." – Henry David Thoreau, Chesuncook, The Main Woods 1848.

Mankind's unconscious error is trading dollars for natural resources and plants and animals that benefit and support the well-being of mankind. Let us find a way to work with this planet before we are all wiped off the face of the earth forever.

What will happen tomorrow, can we control tomorrow? Perhaps the best thing is that tomorrow never happens, we can prevent it from happening by being proactive, by changing our behaviors. We must deal with what is now.

Borders, language, religion, color, wars, what else can divide humanity on this planet. Do we not realize we are all interconnected within this cosmos? There are no borders on this planet. We all share the same world, which is but a tiny island in the cosmos. Do we all consciously want to poison our island? This planet is a tiny island and we have distorted the island to such a point to enhance our convenience, to the detriment of all other things on our island. We no longer look at this island as a place of survival but rather that the island was going to provide no matter how much we take. What a fallacy.

"The sun, the moon and the stars would have disappeared long ago…had they happened to be within the reach of predatory human hands." – Havelock Ellis, The Dance of Life 1923.

Do we not have intelligence to stop? Can we not all live for the benefit of this planet our island to make it a better place for all? The planet now is a sick place, the attitude of wanting more and more needs to go! Life is not a race to accumulate as many things as possible. You cannot take it with you, ask the Pharaohs. We must learn to live as 'one humanity' on a planet to be shared by all.

Our ability to experience life is greater than any other creature; but, instead of experiencing life we are destroying it. We are all slaves, we have been enslaved. We are all joyful willing slaves we have been enslaved by our culture, beliefs, social media, advertisements, work, education, economy, whatever you believe in has been generated for the benefit of an enslaved society. I am willing to do whatever is needed to make money in the world is a wonderful slave, no?

Our behaviors are changing the very face of this planet, the climate, the environment, that the planet has put in place for all life forms, which has taken billions of years we are destroying within our own intelligent life time, the way we do not want. If you do not understand, stand under the hot sun for hours on end, then stand under a tree, even the animals know this, yet we must destroy all trees for profit. Let us destroy the Amazon while we are at it.

In the end, you yourself and the health of the planet you live on is the most important thing, nothing else. Moralistic societies try to do the right things, but nothing right happens within them. We legislate against products and toys that are harmful to humans yet we do not legislate against large corporations that employ thousands of people when they harm the environment. We create the EPA to protect the environment yet are given the powers of a toothless tiger.

We can all see the consequences of our bad behavior toward our planet. We see it unconsciously as we continue with our daily routines.

Behavior does not determine one's consciousness or evolution or one's transformation. We need to become more inclusive, loving nature. Your behavior does not determine who you are. Our behavior toward the planet needs transformation, enlightenment. What does this mean? Who are we as humans, and what roles do we play on this planet.

Society is not just about you it is about everyone and everything around you. The concern is not for you as an individual your concern is for others. If the concern is just about you, then we behave one way. If the concern is for others, we behave another way. This is fundamental and is necessary for planetary transformation and a social consciousness to occur.

If you die tomorrow; think of all things we have accumulated and hang on to with fervor and do not want to lose. Think of the beggar pushing his cart down the street he is hanging on to what little possessions he or she may have, why is that, it's our human nature. Yet, if you knew you had 24 hours to live what would you do? You would give up all your possessions and experience life to the fullest.

Then the question becomes, just, experience life to the fullest enjoyment every day. You need to loosen the hold we have placed on your body, mind, thoughts, and emotions, loosen the hold you have put on yourself. Your life will be transformed. Loosen the hold on everything physical and non-physical. Meditation is being practiced more and more to relieve the stresses of life. The essence of physical existence is change. Nature is changing all the time. The environment is constantly changing. Everything is changing and evolving. Is there anything in nature not changing? Nature is constantly evolving, viruses keep mutating. Physical reality is change. Nothing is constant. If you resist change, you are in essence resisting life. The only place where nothing changes is after we reach the grave. If we resist change, we are resisting the process of life itself which is constantly changing, and the very fundamentals of life's building blocks.

Unfortunately; not accepting change may lead to unhappiness and depression. If you resist change, you resist the whole process of life itself, creating unnecessary worry and depression. The moment we resist change, frustration will occur and then frustration may become depression and it will continue to work against you.

We must get out of our normal lives, we must start to live within nature's boundaries, and we must live with nature not against it. We have an inner mechanism that wants peace, love, harmony, joy and when we interact with nature in a positive manner, we become peaceful and blissful human beings.

However; if, we are employed against nature, and we know in our minds that what we are doing is not good for nature then we psychologically become miserable, worried, anxious, and this becomes our normal lives. We are not happy doing what we are doing. Our mind says one thing our body and our billions of cells are telling us something different. The billions of cells within our body are rebelling against us.

When we work against and threaten nature like cutting down trees. If we work against nature by killing fish, plants, animals and all creatures. When we create chemical poisons, gas and oil, and plastics and dump toxic waste into landfills. Every cell in our body is crying for us to change.

Read that again. Our body, our own cells are telling us what we are doing is causing our own mental distress, our own cancer.

If you are unhappy, time just drags on, if you are joyful time flies by. You are on holiday on a sunny beach with crystal clear waters, the air is full of oxygen yet we only enjoy this for 2 or 3 weeks why? Poof the holiday is over. Why can't life always be like that, what is wrong with that? This; we can do, make the planet a joyful place to live. This we can do! What we are making out of life is the fundamental question. How profoundly do we want to experience life on this planet or do we let it control us? Do we continue to follow social norms just to fit in and exploit the planet to our own self degradation? Do we want trees and greenery and fresh air or do we want steel structures heat, and the stench of gas in the air. Choose!

You are conscious because you know that you are here. We know the world exists but yet we are unconscious to our reality. Does it mean to say we are completely unconscious? No, we are still conscious but not conscious enough to notice the presence of many things. So, consciousness is not whether it is present or absent it is always there. The question is only whether we attain enlightenment of our own conscience. Consciousness is much more than awareness, we are all aware of the perils the world faces with global warming and pollution, we are aware but we continue to act unconsciously as our behaviors have not changed. Government priorities have not changed and will not change until we as humanity become conscious of our interconnectivity with the planet. Measuring economic growth is the wrong measurement. We are still making decisions that are not alleviating future consequences.

To raise consciousness, we need to ask what have we done as a civilization? Our education system has not evolved since reading writing and arithmetic. What happens to children that are musically inclined, they are buried in an archaic system of education. Our education system promotes competitiveness with the only goal is being better than someone else; all team sports are to be the very best at all costs. The only things we enjoy are other people's failures. How can we be conscious of what is happening around us when we are preoccupied being better than everyone else?

The cornerstone of education has been obedience, not developing intelligence about the planet we live on. We need an education system that allows us to question everything. Not just assuming that everything we learn is correct. Change is compulsory. Nature will not allow us to continue on our merry path we need to teach our children about this planet and all the life systems that support it, if we want to change the future it must start with the children.

"You must teach your children that the ground beneath their feet is the ashes of your grandfathers. So that they will respect the land, tell your children that the earth is rich with the lives of our kin. Teach your children what we have taught our children that the earth is our mother. Whatever befalls the earth befalls the sons of the earth. If men spit upon the ground, they spit upon themselves." – Native American Wisdom.

The planet has been here for billions of years it will not wait for us to change. We must institute fundamental change by design not by default.

When you are internally enjoying other people' failures, that is what being number one means I am number one you are not, that is my joy. This is not the way of social consciousness. If from the first day of school you instill this concept in children, how can they possibly develop consciousness? How can we develop awareness for others and for plants and animals and our planet? We have driven consciousness out of ourselves. Scientists and doctors read hundreds of books to become knowledgeable in their field of expertise, yet religious scholars read one book and somehow, they are superior to the rest of us. How can that be? We must start over.

Memory is not intelligence, memory is a capability. Intelligence is different. Consciousness is pure intelligence. We need to look at people, things, animals, plants water, soil, differently. Not as good or bad not as any assigned monetary value, no judgment it just all is. If our intelligence is governed by our memory of the past, we cannot experience a life as it is in the moment. We become judgmental to the detriment of growth and consciousness. Memories build barriers that do not allow us to see our reality. If we cannot see people as they are, we cannot in turn see the plants the animals the sun the trees the flowing blue rivers, the bounty that nature has given us. We are blinded by what we thought we learned to be true yet, our memory deceives us. We have in our heads of memory we have incongruent ideas, and have attached meanings to everything. When there is no meaning. There is no meaning to a sunrise, no meaning to a flower, to a cloud there is no meaning to anything. We as humans try to attach meanings to everything, just enjoy what is!

The millions of cells within the body retain every bit of ancient memory. Do you want to use your whole body or just the mental memories that sit on your shoulders and in your head? This is the difference between being fully conscious or just partially aware which includes all of the things which are blocking your consciousness. That memory, education, religion, political biases all these things do not permit you to use your full conscious ability. If you read 1,000 books and remember all of them, the value you have is only the memory you have. What kind of human being am I, is our only true value. Whatever memories you carry in your mind, has little value.

This is a great time for humanity and as human beings. When we were only concerned with survival, we could not pay attention to any of the other dimensions of life. Any other creature on the planet, if their stomachs are full, they are peaceful. Just sleep in the fields and enjoy life. When the human stomach is full, we have 1,000 problems. Our lives are no longer fulfilled with survival. When this is threatened, we are just like any other animal. When our stomach is full, we become even more voracious to everything around us. We should be making the world a better place yet we are not, we are using our past memories and intelligence to destroy the very life systems that support us.

When you realize; you were born to die, it is only a question of time and time is ticking away and we let it tick away into nothingness. Is that what we want? We are moving closer to our death, yet if you are conscious that you are mortal, we would organize our limited time on this planet in the most productive way possible and live with the beauty of nature.

People are trying to be politically correct, say the right words, do the right thing and fit into social norms. Is everyone so screwed up in their heads, we push social issues to a level of paranoia. Can we no longer hug children, talk to them about all types of important planetary issues?

We are exercising only one dimension of our intelligence which is our intellect. We love to analyze things to the nth degree, and we open and dissect things. If I want to know you better, it is like dissecting a frog, do I now know you better, and do we now know frogs better? Perhaps their biology, but we do not really know them, do we? Dissecting that is what we do to know things what makes things tic. We really know nothing about nature, yet dissecting is what we do and what is taught in biology class, oh well another frog has been sacrificed for our education that we will never use again. By including animals, man will know them much better by dissecting them, but what have we learned in the lab? We are trying to apply this method to our own lives, and I can tell you it will not work. The more educated the more disturbed we have become. Education should enhance the beauty of life. Educated people should have been the solution, but educated people are the problem. We you and I are the problem. We are using rudimentary tools like intellect from memory. It is the story of our humanity.

Are we paying attention to every aspect of life? From childhood our minds are taken away from the focus of nature. Information that we learn gives us a false feeling that we know everything. Anyone who wants to navigate thru any situation needs intelligence not just information, but we act on information without using our intelligence and our consciousness.

What is the uniqueness about being human? Information is useful but we need intelligence. Mother Nature and the planet have much more power than us. A billion years more power than our puny 200 years of industrialization. Intelligence will allow us to navigate through any situation. Once we accumulate too much information then we no longer pay attention to what is around us and we lose our ability to access our intelligence. We will just repeat information from our memories.

Consciousness is the basis of human life. Whatever is imagined in your mind can be manifested in the world. Consciousness is the most important element of the mind, memory less so. We must explore new possibilities, in our experience not just economic ventures, which is what is shaping our experience right now. How do human beings live on this planet in concert with the rhythms of the planet? Our growth is limited by our memories and identification of an ideology within these memories. The more we attach ourselves to our memories the less effective we become. Today a child through the internet can name a galaxy, light years away but of what value is this for the child.

We need to do what is needed now. Life is phenomena beyond our comprehension. How could basic matter such as atoms, protons, neutrons and other materials develop into the billions of life forms that exist? It is beyond our comprehension of what nature itself can create. We need common sense and sensitivity as life on this planet is inter-connected, woven from the same basic elements. We as humanity have evolved a little further than our ape cousins and have lost other lines of evolution along the path of self-recognition. Yet we are destroying our/their habitat for what? Our own convenience which if we continue will lead to our own self destruction. If all the humans die, the planet will once again become vibrant and flourish. Is this what we want? Can we not co-exist with all the life that has been created on this planet? That is the question. The most destructive idea that we have generated in our minds through education, religion, is that creation is human centric. At one time, we believed the earth was the center of the universe, how wrong we were.

We are against animals or creatures that can eat us, that can eat our crops, eat our farm animals, yet all these animals, insects are important for a vibrant planet. We as humans create pesticides to destroy insects. Birds and bats eat insects and because we have poisoned them, we are also poisoning and killing the very creatures we love. Pesticides kill bees that pollinate our flowers our crops our food without bees we have no food. Why do I no longer hear the magnificent echo of song birds?

The concept of a shifting baseline reflects on the fact that young people forget about what happened in the past. If something is changing, for example the abundance of wild animals and bio-diversity in general. People are aware of what is there only when they wake up to the world, this is baseline they will use to assess change. They are aware of what has changed in their lifetime when they are old. They are not aware of what has changed before in the life time of their predecessors. So you have a situation where people are aware of the changes that have happened in their lifetime, but not of the changes that have occurred before. So the baseline that is used to assess change is itself changing. This leads to the gradual accommodation of impoverishment of biodiversity. To the reduced abundance of plants, animals, soil water, around us. This is a gradual loss of diversity against which we cannot do anything because we do not notice it. (Ref: Dr. Daniel Pauly).

Christopher Columbus's log book 'Approaching Cuba we saw turtles 3 to 4 feet long in such vast numbers that they covered the sea'. No one alive today can imagine a scene like that. More than 95% of the sea turtles are gone from the planet. We destroyed most of their habitat. We are forgetting how things use to look and how they should look. We have lost millions of birds in such a short amount of time. Natives talk of the salmon returning to rivers every year. There was so many you could walk along their backs to cross the river. What have we done? There was plenty for all and now with our knowledge and intelligence we are creating less and less for everyone.

The planet is one, we are all interconnected. The planet has no boundaries, rivers flow freely from country to country. The air blows freely, the oceans rise and fall with no borders. Life is all connected, yet we do not see it. Humanity we are all the same. All the problems we are facing are within our control.

We need to transform our roles on this planet from unconscious behavior to a conscious behavior.

"This is a beautiful planet and not all fragile. Earth can withstand significant volcanic eruptions, tectonic cataclysms, and ice ages. But this canny, intelligent, prolific, and extremely self-centered human creature has proven himself capable of more destruction of life than Mother Nature herself. We've got to be stopped." – Michael l. Fischer Harper's July 1990 stopped.

Chapter 6
Global Behavior and
Unconsciousness

Socrates loved the pursuit of wisdom more than any other. He valued truth, understanding, and examination of self and life above all else. He believed that the most valuable thing a person could do was question their thoughts, beliefs, and perceived truths. For Socrates, the examined life was the only life worth living.

Even if you know little-to-nothing about Socrates, you have probably heard the famous dictum which states that *'The unexamined life is not worth living'*. Socrates apparently made this pronouncement at his trial, essentially choosing death over exile. Classical Wisdom.

We are all one with the planet, but we are all unconscious to this fact. This is the only truth we all need to know.

What is the greatest problem of our life? What is the greatest benefit? It is that our intelligence has turned against us. It has created stress, anxiety, tension, depression, misery, and in the end madness. Our intelligence has turned against us. Our intelligence is not working for us it is working against us. We have become unconscious. We have lost our social consciousness with our own environment on this planet. We are working against ourselves. Unlike any other creature, we can change and evolve consciously. Subconsciously we all know inherently what is bad and what is good. We have lost our compass we have lost our morality compass. We need to find it again for all of humanity and the fragile world we live on.

We are the just the wrong intelligence for this planet. It is time to figure out why we have intelligence. Is it not a sad story being the most evolved creature on this planet? Our level of intelligence has deceived us. As we continue to be led by industrialists and leaders that are like war mongers. It has taken us millions of years of evolution to get us to this point in the history of mankind. The next step will determine the final outcome of humanity. We are at our peak of intelligence, yet we destroy everything in our path. We want to be at the top of the world, we want it all. Are we creating happiness? We create only misery for millions on this planet because it is never enough. Some have it all to the detriment of everyone and everything else.

The planet will unleash its own virus, which will keep changing as we try to outsmart it. If we do not change, our treatment of this planet we will no longer be on this planet.

The world population is clearly out of control, populations and cultures capitalized on each other's discoveries, the medical discoveries soon led to higher birth rates, longer lives and over population. If we can increase life expectancy, should we not postpone birth? Humanity will suffocate on its own unsustainable growth. The life-giving waters will become more polluted, with chemicals of all sorts, fertilizers and pharmaceuticals, so much so we will spawn new unimagined molecular life forms. We are changing the very chemistry of life changing not slowly but very rapidly into the unknown of our own un-relentless pursuit of economic and industrial growth.

"The command be fruitful and multiply was promulgated according to our authorities when the population of the world consisted of two people." – William Ralph Inge More Lay—Thoughts of a Dean. 1931.

Humanity is trapped by our own cultural upbringing. It is an animal instinct, the survival of species. Now the survival of the race depends on controlling populations without war and conflict. In 1910, the world population was 1.58 billion, today it is 7.6 billion and ever increasing.

*"14 May 2018, the United States Census Bureau calculated the world population as 7,472,985,269 for that same date and the United Nations estimated over 7 billion. In 2017, the United Nations increased the medium variant projections to **9.8 billion for 2050** and 11.2 billion for 2100."*

At a population of 10–11 billion, who will want to remain on this planet devoid of everything if we continue down the path we are on? With an ever-increasing rise in world population, we are ensuring that our children cannot live well on this planet. We are producing more children and increasing our life expectancies. Humans use to live to some 30 years of age now the life expectancy is well passed 70 or 80 years if age.

11 billion people consuming everything on earth at the rate of US consumption of material things is a warning to all intelligent beings. In the early 19th century, life expectancy started to increase in the early industrialized countries while it stayed low in the rest of the world...Since 1900, **the global average life expectancy has more than doubled** and is now above 70 years.

That means there are many more people living on the planet who are living twice as long. If we do not consciously contain the population, nature will do it in a very cruel way. Do you want to wait for that day? If we do it consciously, we can achieve an optimal population balance.

All people want all the material conveniences of the countries that are causing the most pollution. We are outstripping and out eating everything on this planet. Can we agree on a solution without a world war to reduce our population? Has our intelligence reached such maturity? Reducing world population is a plausible solution. We all help each other so there is no need to conquer one another to and to assimilate ideologies.

We continue to be the parasite on this planet if we do not take care of ourselves nature will, and outbreaks in nature do not end well.

We are running out of fresh water, by creating dams to preserve water we have less water in the ground to support the plants and trees that hold water and hold the ground and prevent desertification. We consciously take water areas to grow more agricultural areas. We are running out of water, we cause global warming by continuously spewing CO_2 and methane into the atmosphere, by growing industries. We continue to produce products that contain plastics that are discarded into nature; they poison our oceans and our fish. We are using more resources than can be replenished naturally. We are operating at a very unconscious level to what is happening around us.

How did we come down this path, destroying our world, our environment little by little and kill all the animals, the lack of greenery, the lack of clean water for all? Industrialization—the work for money concept, placing a value on all living things (how inhumane) buy more products that deplete resources, pollute water put plastics in the water. We are caught in our "web of entanglement".

Did you know plastics take 5,000 years to decompose that is over 50 generations let me repeat that if fish eat plastics and die there will be 50 generations with no fish. Have you seen the awful pictures of sea creatures struggling to swim with plastic netting around their fins and gills, trying to move with a plastic bottle trapped in the netting? Have you seen divers trying to remove many plastic netting caught on a whale's fin and could not swim? This is happening today. Fish eat the tiny plastics thinking it is food, plastic mimic plankton. They die from the plastic then the birds eat the fish and they die from the plastic. There is plastic everywhere when will we stop? When will we stop destroying nature and ourselves?

Deforestation, putting gas in the air using the cars we need to work. We put toxic soap with all the clothes we wash in our drinking water. We destroy then we forget how it was before. Remember we could drink from the cold rivers that ran in the country side. The wells were not polluted. Over 70% of the land is used for agriculture, which itself is killing bio diversity. 85% of earth's forest have been cleared, now they want to clear the Amazon, we are losing the lungs of the planet, we are killing ourselves.

Looking at the big picture, the world is just one tiny planet in a huge solar system in a huge cosmos that extends forever. This tiny planet which has been here for billions of years which contains all that is necessary to support life has created trees and plants to exhale oxygen, oceans of water that has spawned life. It is this planet, this environment that has spawned our intelligence or stupidity from billions of years of slow evolution and diversity. We are part of the process we all have different cultures that have been created by our environments by our memories and beliefs. We are the pinnacle of creation we have evolved with our intelligence; we can communicate in many languages. Yet we still do not fully understand all plants and animal communication. We are insensitive to humanity and our own kind. We lack compassion for other cultures and for all the creatures that inhabit this planet.

We are curious creatures; we continuously ask why? Why is, what is? We a long time ago had an awakening all over the planet. We evolved our thought process even more. We identified with idols, the god of thunder, and the god of the sun, and on and on. We questioned further and scientifically identified what caused thunder, and that the sun was a very large burning planet in the sky. Once we thought the earth was the center of the universe.

In order to evolve, we must understand the past, not fix the past into our memories, because what we remember and what is may be two very different things. Ever play telephone message, try it get a group of 10–20 people and pass a message to the first person and then ask that person to tell the message word for word to the next person mouth to mouth till it reaches the last person. Then that person tells the message to the group you will find it is no longer that same original message it was enhanced or changed in some way but was different than the original message. That is memory what one remembers and sees is very different from someone else. Yet we hang on to our memories as if they were life or death. It is time to let go and start over.

Once we recognize this, that it is only necessary to know the past, and by knowing the past we can forget the past. We can evolve to a new future which says humanity is all one with itself and all creation on this planet. We are one with the powerful creation of this environment that has spawned humanity. Why would we; with our intelligence, want to willingly continue to destroy our environment?

Why is this important? All books ever written were written by man that is a truth. We have divided ourselves by what we have written whatever we believe has been created by man. We must release ourselves from the chains of the past if we have any chance of moving forward.

Me vs. the planet is a very bad concept, we will not win. It is extremely reckless to continue exploiting the planet for our own personal benefit that leads to the destruction of our life supporting environment. If we are not in sync with the flow and ebb of the planet, we humanity becomes the virus. It is not a competition we want to get into, the result will not turn out well for humanity. Economic growth and conditioning are the infections that blind all of us. It is not our living reality. The world is a fragile planet a bio sphere in space, yet we attack it with impunity as if we can continue on as if there will be no consequences.

"The earth we abuse and the living things we kill will, in the end, for in exploiting their presence we are diminishing our future." – Marya Mannes, More in Anger, 1958.

We are still breathing we are transacting with the planet, but why do we put out more poisonous gas than the planet can dissipate? Why destroy ourselves? Why do we do that, for profit? It is madness. It is unconscious insanity.

We are part of the planet, because we have reached intelligence, we think we can manipulate the planet only to our benefit, which has become our detriment. In 200 years of industrialization, what have we done as a species to improve the planet, that which supports all life. What have we done to add value to the planet? Nothing significant we only take away and give back very little.

Our very existence is a constant engagement with the planet. But our very intelligent minds see the planet as an opportunity for profit and put us directly in conflict with nature, and we will not win. If we continue to maintain the competition against the planet, what will be our outcome? Who will win? In 200 years, we have succeeded in taking everything nature has given us at no cost to us. Yet we continue to destroy everything that has gotten us to this point of natural selection. The planet has been here for billions of years building an environment for all creatures. Humanity has been here for over 200,000 years (Ref: Universetoday.com), with the last 200 being the most devastating to this planet. We come into this planet with nothing, and we will leave with nothing yet we turn our homes into warehouse of goods that when the end comes no one will want your stuff. We have all been conditioned, programmed by advertising to have more than everyone else. We must have the latest gizmo, the latest gadget. Why? Do we really need 3 or 4 cars that pump carbon dioxide into the air?

We have been conditioned by our upbringing, our education, by our parents who want their children to have more than they did. By corporations that have an endless thirst for profit regardless of the harm they cause, the environment is but a casualty on their path to profitability. We have been conditioned by our own economic growth that is unsustainable.

We are unfortunately the wrong intelligence for this planet. Why did the universe give us intelligence only to destroy the very source of our lives? We can change to be gardeners and caretakers of this planet or we can continue to be plunderers. Right now, we are plunderers and the planet will treat us like the virus we are. All this must change if we are to survive, we need to be caretakers of the planet, of ourselves and each other. We must move from our unconscious behaviors to attain a higher level of consciousness in planetary awareness.

The biggest mistake humanity is making is to believe we can continue to keep doing what we are doing and change nothing. To continue economic growth with the false hope of prosperity, yet we continue spewing emissions in the air and put poisons in the ground, contaminate and decimate the oceans by overfishing, chemicals and plastics. Climate catastrophe is upon us from everything that we are doing. The water we drink the air we breathe; it is all one planet, a microcosm there is no place on earth you can hide.

Our endless march to economic growth of wealth and profitability cannot continue.

We are one with the planet; we are all interconnected, if we continue the planet will rebel against us in unimaginable ways. The more and more we try to manipulate this planet to benefit of only ourselves, the worse off the next generations will be. We act as if we are the only thing that matters on this planet. By doing this to our benefit, it is actually to our own detriment. We now have to face our consequences whether we like it or not. We have to face these consequences through our own vast knowledge of stupidity and unconsciousness.

"We do not inherit the earth from our ancestors; we borrow it from our children." – Native American Proverb.

The viruses will become common occurrence is just one of the measures nature is throwing at us, the more damage we cause to nature the more it will rebel against us. There will be more floods, famine, heat and fire as we continue to cut trees for profit and agriculture and living. The more we try to manipulate the planet only for our benefit the more the nature will react in a very negative way toward humanity. We must change or future generations will face a very uncertain future.

Can we use this time to change our ugliness, can we turn in a different direction and finally recognize that having an endless economy without regards to the effects on nature and our own existence is the path of self-destruction. As we destroy everything around us to make our lives more comfortable, we are also destroying our own future generations. Can we not see it?

What we are doing is wrong for all of us. We are unconscious as we choose a blind eye and continue on. This unconscious behavior is happening all over the planet. To have a better life we need to gather material things that we will not take with us to our graves. Yet the planet cannot support the life styles everyone wants. We must *consciously* change our behavior.

As humans we have become self-destructive. The technology which is supposed to make our lives beautiful and easy has become the source of all world problems. We are in the slow yet ever increasing source of all the climactic problems. What should have been a boon to mankind has become a curse.

"The system of nature, of which man is a part, tends to be self-balancing, self-adjusting, self-cleansing. Not so with technology." – E.F. Schumacher, Small is Beautiful 1973.

What has brought incredible level of comfort and convenience to humanity in the last 100—200 years has become a threat to all our lives. We have disconnected with our life source. What gives us life, the planet, the water, the air, the earth, the plants and animals the bio diversity of the wondrous nature. We have lost our way. Unless human beings open up our *consciousness* to what is happening around us, we will never resolve the humanitarian calamity that will befall upon us. Right now, for most humans we do not experience nor understand the life source we are a very part of. It is us against the planet and what is in it for me!

We must consciously obliterate our individualities, our ego centric views. If we do not do this, we will never achieve the level of *consciousness* that is required to revolutionize our purpose on this planet. Our purpose is not to be in conflict with the planet but rather to be in harmony. Survival of the fittest is no longer the mantra, but rather survival for all of us. The past has not worked; we must do something else radically different.

This is the time to raise human **'unconsciousness to consciousness'** our window of opportunity is upon us now. This is the generation's time to act; do we have the courage and commitment to change the destiny of humanity on this planet?

"Forgive them for they know not what they do." – Jesus.

"Oh beautiful for smoggy skies, insecticide grains, for strip-mined mountain's majesty above the asphalt plain. America, America, man sheds his waste on thee, and hides the pines with billboards signs, from sea to oily sea" – George Carlin.

Chapter 7
Why Do We Work

This might be an existential question. But where did work come from? Who benefits most from work? Do we enjoy the work we do? It may be a stupid question, but a fundamentally important one.

How long can men thrive between walls of brick, walking on asphalt pavements, breathing coal and of oil, growing, working, dying, with hardly a thought of wind, and sky and fields of grain, seeing only manmade machinery, the mineral-like quality of life? Charles Lindberg, Readers Digest Nov 1939.

We are born to work, for others in poisonous sweat factories, metal structures that were built displacing trees and that will rot as time goes by *'our gift to the industrialization of our planet'.* We are born to feed large factories to produce products that are extracted and made from the nature of life that made us the intelligence we are. Or are we?

People are preoccupied, their minds are busy. Their lives are controlled by their thoughts and emotions. We are working, but there are a lot of problems within ourselves. Every day we are struggling with our own internal psychological issues. Right to the end of our lives we are still struggling with the same things. We can live life with ease but, people think that to be successful they must work hard. If we work hard, life will be tedious and we will work even harder to earn a little extra. The problem is we should be enjoying our work with ease. If not, then life becomes a struggle. People are earning a living reproducing and dying nothing more. This is all we are doing, nothing more. We are eating, working, sleeping, reproducing, and living unconsciously. Every other creature on this planet does the same thing without having the intelligence that we have. Yet they achieve the same thing without harming their environment. No. we must work joyfully, and how do we work joyfully? Everyone has to grow up and get a job, I must get a job. Why? We study to learn skills that will allow us to earn income. How many years do we spend to learn a trade? We go to school, university, work specialization, now 20 years of our lives has passed, more or less. Now we get the job we want and we work from the age of 20 to 65 even longer, in poor countries the children are made to work to produce product cheaply for the rest of the world. In the modern world, you may spend one to two hours sometimes or more in traffic going to and from your work. We have billions of gas vehicles spewing tons of carbon dioxide in the atmosphere. Do you know how much atmosphere this planet has? The average height of the troposphere is 13 km (8.1 mi) there is where most of the oxygen is. We have 13 km or 8 miles that separates us from non-breathable gases. Does that not worry you as we spew tons of poisonous gases into the atmosphere? Will there be a tipping of the balance. We are undoing billions of years of planetary evolution. Yet, we sit in our vehicles for 1 or 2 hours sometimes more, poisoning ourselves. Ever keep a car running in a closed-door garage, how long will a person survive? Leaving a car running in a closed garage will produce enough carbon monoxide to overcome and kill a person within a few minutes. A few minutes in universal time are nothing. Yet our intelligence fails us. We continue to spew billions of tons of poisonous gas into the atmosphere, all the while cutting the trees and plants that absorb this gas. The planet will become our garage and the doors are closing. Did you know the atmosphere on our planet is like the size of the peel of a tomato; that's it and we are changing this atmosphere to our own peril.

I need to make money to buy useless things and, in the end, we cannot load containers and take it with us, it is left to pollute nature. Cargo ships are spilling containers as we speak into the ocean polluting ocean life as we speak. At a very young age, we are asked; what do you want to be when you grow up? We are already conditioning our children to a life of constant work and no enjoyment of nature. Nature is oblivious around us. I apologize we do enjoy it, two weeks of vacation we venture to where pure nature is unspoiled by humanity, unspoiled forests, unspoiled mountains, unspoiled oceans and seas. The question becomes why can we not enjoy pure nature and life for 52 weeks? What is holding us back? Why must we spoil nature right where we live? Why?

I have a job, now we are all on autopilot. (Automatic mode of work), I live to work. Working for 50 years to enjoy life for two weeks or a month out of the year is not living. I have a job I do not have to think anymore. I do not want to be conscious of what is happening around me. My life is taken care of. No! It is a trap. This is not the way to live.

People live for the one and only purpose of earning as much money as possible in order to be able to buy as many things as possible. It is not surprising those discussions about potential solutions to fight global warming concentrate on technical solutions instead of fundamental changes in how we live.

Somewhere during the industrial revolution work for pay has led to consumerism. Do we need to work? If we want to maintain our life styles as we are told we must continue to work, but who has told us this? The advertisers of huge corporations who spend billions of dollars to get consumers to buy, you see the signs everywhere, bombarded by ads on TV. Then we retire at 65 or not and how much of life is left? Not much, and you spent 45–50 years working. To retire in comfort surrounded by material things that were purchased by the money you earned working, and you cannot take anything with you, is it not better to enjoy life, enjoy friendship, care and giving than buying?

Does a million dollars make you happy, does a billion? Does it really matter when life around you is crumbling? Work makes us mentally challenged. We are so focused and absorbed in our work environment we become slaves to it, we fail to see the larger picture without any clarity. We become puppets on a shoestring.

"Today's worst addictions are not marijuana, cocaine or even alcohol. They are the addictions to money and self, and in the relentless pursuit of self-satisfaction, it is often children who are the casualties." – Frank Jones.

I would hasten to say 85% of us do not enjoy what we do. Most people hate what they do, but spend most of their lives doing it, trying to convince themselves that they love their jobs. If you are slaving away for retirement or wealth accumulation or a better life; we are all missing the point. Only roughly 80% of people reach the age of 65. After 65, on average you have 15 more years to live. Approximately 65 % of people reach the age of 80. We must re-invent ourselves, what we always wanted to be in concert with beauty of nature. But we say I have a family to feed, a bank loan to pay, a mortgage to pay. Think of it this way, if you work for 40 years, of course your children will follow in your footsteps and will fall into the work trap. Do we want a fulfilled life a life full of wonder and amazement of this our only planet. Even if we make less money, it does not matter how much money we make. We all die in the end, and it does not matter. We must re-think our lives and reach a higher level of consciousness to get us out of this vicious circle we have created for ourselves. Why must we continue if we are not happy in our work? We must re-think what we are doing; re-think our purpose, our meaning in our lives. We must change it! It is okay to make less money, doing something we love and not feel the need to buy more of everything that we did not really need. Do we really need a new car, just because our friend has one?

Does it not follow that as humans we get greatest pleasure for giving than taking? Yet every day the corporations pay us to take away more and more from the environment of this planet. We know; each one of us knows, we are paid to do the environmentally wrong things. Why? We need money for food, clothing, and rent with the rest we buy lots and lots of stuff.

We work for a meager pay, we toil 5 or more days a week, perhaps 2 or more jobs just to make ends meet. We are slaves we have been conditioned to this economic environment. How?

We are conditioned by advertisements to buy more to buy bigger to buy better. We borrow from the banks (who also borrow and invest in oil and gas corporations to increase their profits) and now we have a car loan, a house loan with a 25-year mortgage, a student loan, a holiday loan. All these loans we need to work more, the more we work the more taxes we pay because our government debts are out of control. Do we not see this vicious circle? We are all entangled in the mess we have created our own 'Web of Entanglement'. If some significant event occurs, we cannot change the direction of our lives. Let me repeat that, you cannot change the direction of your life. This is a slave's life. We are stuck unable to change because of our own debt. We have built this web. Long term financial obligations keep us enslaved right where we are. Unable to move, unable to decide right from wrong, we are entangled in our own web working for 50 years as a slave to others as we destroy our health. **Our environment is our wealth it is in the trees in the animals and nature around us, it is in the soil in the water and in the air.**

Why are people suffering in a world of plenty? Workers are not being treated with dignity. Company leaders have no moral standards and the environment, pollution and global warming is not their priority. We require regulation so that greed cannot continue to run amok. We need to make these false LEADERS in government and industry accountable for their inaction toward the prosperity of this planet. Billions of dollars are hoarded by the very few and yet countless hundreds of thousands of our little children and homeless adults live in poverty. That is moral indignation, which has gotten us to where we are.

Have you noticed how times have changed, we use to believe we would work for one organization all of our lives, live the good life. How times have changed. The middle class is being eliminated as corporations seek more profit, they move the middle-class jobs offshore for meager pay. Soon there will be no middle-class worker. Middle class is being displaced by automation, outsourcing, computers, and robots. Middle class is now working as travel guides, housekeepers, social workers, medical assistants, and hostesses. These are all low skill low wages. It is painful to see the middleclass jobs disappear as top company executive rake in millions for their cost saving efforts and sales. Sales because we the middle class are still buying the crap they are selling. This is the disparity of the future we are all faced with. Low paying jobs and unemployment. (Data The American middle class at the end of an Era)

What is missing is compassion toward all humanity on the planet we live. We are in a self-induced plague, rents are becoming unaffordable, and food is becoming unaffordable, all for profit. Housing is unaffordable. This is why government must legislate against runaway costs of food, housing and basic needs. We have lost our social responsibility as a nation as a country to the planet we live on.

"You forget that the fruits belong to all and that the land belongs to no one." – Jean Jacques Rousseau, Discours sur l'origine et les fondements de l'inégalité parmis les homes, 1755.

We start with a planet and we assume infinite resources. Definition of Assume: "Ass out of you and me." We have financial institutions that will borrow money to anyone who has a job or assets. Government have asset, and lots of land, they give away these lands to industrialists to mine, to extract minerals, to extract water, to extract gas, to extract oil, to remove forests, for profits these corporations hire people for pay to do their dirty work to poison the land. We the people the slaves comply. Why do we comply, we have families to support we have debts to pay, we are all caught in this **'web of entanglement'**. Somewhere I read that there are approximately 6.5 million US households that are behind in their rental payments, collectively owing more than US 20 billion to landlords and banks.

Humanity has lost its sense of perception, we are not seeing things as they are, and corporations manipulate our thoughts, government and our lives with greedy smiles.

These corporations have no regard for nature they are there just to extract a profit, and the government allows it because they need the revenue from the taxes to pay their debt. These corporations have false advertising to promote and sell their products, false advertising regarding the damage they cause, they pay the politicians political campaign to gain their favor to enact laws to circumvent the damage they cause to the environment, which the people need just to live.

What are people's lives committed to? The majority of people are committed to themselves our own egos which are expressed in the accumulation of money and material things. Their psychological needs, their emotional needs their physical needs are all connected to ego. We work in business, we have a career, family, home, these are all pre-arranged for you to work the rest of your lives as slaves to industry that is undermining the planet. We are all in a vicious 'web of entanglement'.

With all of our debts, government, household, personal, it enslaves us forever. It is here to serve you or you to serve them? Humans serve them their entire life and are unconscious. Food, shelter, security and this is called a normal life. We must become abnormal. We must use our lives to enjoy our lives to the enhancement of this life; not to the enslavement of this life. Economy and debt are man-made, where is the real wealth? Is it in money, is it in material things? Or is it in the beauty of nature and all living things. That is where true wealth is. We do not have to keep up with the Joneses. Forget about job titles. Don't look back at the end of your life and see unfulfilled dreams, years that were just wasted away in a job that we hate. Your mind is saying the pay is great but every cell in your body is telling you this job is not environmentally sound and I am destroying nature. That is why you hate your job. We are so busy working that we forget to make a happy life.

Life is so short, do something that you love in sync with nature. Be able to spend time with people you love. You were not born just to pay bills and die. We are born to enjoy life. To its fullest and be in sync with nature. Think about when were your happiest experiences, when you are near nature, the ocean, the mountains, the fields of green. Why is it so stress free? I ask why do we work our lives and toil for others for 50 years and then life is over. What have you accomplished? Is this your life? We can change and not work for others but rather replenishing our energy by giving back to the planet making this time this era this planet a better place for everyone. When will we see life as it is? When? In this struggle we have forgotten to live our lives. There are lives that have not been lived at all. We are dragging ourselves from one stage of life to another without experiencing the life around you. Life will pass away in front of our eyes. I forgot to live life because we did not see it. To enjoy my life with all that was given to us on this planet.

In third world countries, people live in the bush off the land who fish and farm and hunt and who live in environmentally friendly huts. We classified them as poor, but are they? Do they work for a living or do they just enjoy life, like birds. Do they destroy nature or live with it? Think about it, really think about it. They are living with nature not destroying it. They were enjoying life till corporations told them they were not.

An American mythology, "People are rich because of hard work, but nobody can explain why those who work hard have no money," They work to spend.

No one is asking fundamental questions—What is life? Who am I, why am I who I am? What is the nature of our existence? We must change the way we live to become conscious about ourselves and our fundamental being on this planet. Do we all want to continue to destroy it? Do we?

"Our complex global economy is built upon millions of small, private acts of psychological surrender, the willingness of people to acquiesce in playing their assigned parts as cogs in the great social machine that encompasses all other machines. The capacity for self-enslavement must be broken." – Theodore Roszak, The Voice of the Earth.

Chapter 8
Unconsciousness of Our Own Planet

We are totally ignorant about the lives of other plants animals and creatures that live around us. In fact, we do not even care about our own kind that lives on this planet. As long as there are wars, we remain intelligent barbarians. If everyone lived by this cardinal rule, we would all be so much better off. "Love your neighbor and all living things as you love yourself. "We fall seriously short of loving our own species let alone all the other plant and creatures that nature has provided for on this planet. Billions of years of evolution will be destroyed by a ravenous creature with intelligence but no conscious."

How many symbiotic relationships do you know? It is everywhere in nature, two different kinds of species living with or near each other in a symbiotic relationship that normally benefits both species, but not always. The most common is the flower and the bee, and there are many more. Did you know humans have a mutual relationship with microorganisms, primarily bacteria, in their digestive tract? Bacteria aid in the digestion and regulate the intestinal environment, and they in turn feed off the foods humans eat. There are so many things happening within and around ourselves but we do not see them with any clarity. We are clueless to the billions of years that nature has taken to create the planet we live on. We are unconscious to the planet that has created us and the interconnectivity of all the life that surrounds. We are connected to this life, but we act as if we are the creator, and are intoxicated by our beliefs of which we know nothing.

It shames me when authorities kill coyotes that live in the wilderness at Stanley Park, Vancouver BC. The coyote has nipped at the heel of some teenager that is in their habitat disturbing the coyotes. With signs clearly stating, "Do not enter Coyotes" Why do we shoot the coyotes, we have taken all their land should we not discipline the intelligent human that purposefully went to antagonize them. Will we kill all predators till there are none left, sharks, lions, wolves? We do not understand the relationship all these creatures have with the planet culling the sick, the weak, and prevents illnesses from spreading in nature.

Do Trees Talk to Each Other?

A controversial German forester says yes, and his ideas are shaking up the scientific world article below by Richard Grant March 2018.

From the book 'The Hidden Life of Trees: What They Feel, How They Communicate' by Peter Wohlleben.

"We don't ask questions about the interconnectedness of the forest, Are trees social beings? In this international bestseller, forester and author Peter Wohlleben convincingly makes the case that, yes, the forest is a social network."

"Since Darwin, we have generally thought of trees as striving, disconnected loners, competing for water, nutrients and sunlight, with the winners shading out the losers and sucking them dry. The timber industry in particular sees forests as wood-producing systems and battlegrounds for survival of the fittest."

There is now a substantial body of scientific evidence that refutes that idea. It shows instead that trees of the same species are communal, and will often form alliances with trees of other species. Forest trees have evolved to live in cooperative, interdependent relationships, maintained by communication and a collective intelligence similar to an insect colony. These soaring columns of living wood draw the eye upward to their outspreading crowns, but the real action is taking place underground, just a few inches below our feet.

"Some are calling it the 'wood-wide web'," says Wohlleben. "All the trees here, and in every forest that is not too damaged, are connected to each other through underground fungal networks. Trees share water and nutrients through the networks, and also use them to communicate. They send distress signals about drought and disease, or insect attacks, and other trees alter their behavior when they receive these messages."

Scientists call these mycorrhizal networks. The fine, hair like root tips of trees join together with microscopic fungal filaments to form the basic links of the network, which appears to operate as a symbiotic relationship between trees and fungi, or perhaps an economic exchange.

The fungi consume about 30 percent of the sugar that trees photosynthesize from sunlight. The sugar is what fuels the fungi, as they scavenge the soil for nitrogen, phosphorus and other mineral nutrients, which are then absorbed and consumed by the trees.

For young saplings in a deeply shaded part of the forest, the network is literally a lifeline. Lacking the sunlight to photosynthesize, they survive because big trees, including their parents, pump sugar into their roots through the network. Wohlleben likes to say that mother trees 'suckle their young', which both stretches a metaphor and gets the point across vividly.

Once, he came across a gigantic beech stump in this forest, four or five feet across. The tree was felled 400 or 500 years ago, but scraping away the surface with his penknife, Wohlleben found something astonishing: the stump was still green with chlorophyll. There was only one explanation. The surrounding beeches were keeping it alive, by pumping sugar to it through the network. "When beeches do this, they remind me of elephants," he says. "They are reluctant to abandon their dead, especially when it's a big, old, revered matriarch."

To communicate through the network, trees send chemical, hormonal and slow-pulsing electrical signals, which scientists are just beginning to decipher. Edward Farmer at the University of Lausanne in Switzerland has been studying the electrical pulses, and he has identified a voltage-based signaling system that appears strikingly similar to animal nervous systems (although he does not suggest that plants have neurons or brains). Alarm and distress appear to be the main topics of tree conversation, although Wohlleben wonders if that's all they talk about. "What do trees say when there is no danger and they feel content? This I would love to know." Monica Gagliano at the University of Western Australia has gathered evidence that some plants may also emit and detect sounds, and in particular, a crackling noise in the roots at a frequency of 220 hertz, inaudible to humans.

Trees also communicate through the air, using pheromones and other scent signals. Wohlleben's favorite example occurs on the hot, dusty savannas of sub-Saharan Africa, where the wide-crowned umbrella thorn acacia is the emblematic tree. When a giraffe starts chewing acacia leaves, the tree notices the injury and emits a distress signal in the form of ethylene gas. Upon detecting this gas, neighboring acacias start pumping tannins into their leaves. In large enough quantities, these compounds can sicken or even kill large herbivores.

Giraffes are aware of this, however, having evolved with acacias, and this is why they browse into the wind, so the warning gas doesn't reach the trees ahead of them. If there's no wind, a giraffe will typically walk 100 yards— farther than ethylene gas can travel in still air—before feeding on the next acacia. Giraffes, you might say, know that the trees are talking to one another.

Trees can detect scents through their leaves, which, for Wohlleben, qualify as a sense of smell. They also have a sense of taste. When elms and pines come under attack by leaf-eating caterpillars, for example, they detect the caterpillar saliva, and release pheromones that attract parasitic wasps. The wasps lay their eggs inside the caterpillars, and the wasp larvae eat the caterpillars from the inside out. "Very unpleasant for the caterpillars," says Wohlleben. "Very clever of the trees."

A recent study from Leipzig University and the German Centre for Integrative Biodiversity Research shows that trees know the taste of deer saliva. "When a deer is biting a branch, the tree brings defending chemicals to make the leaves taste bad," he says. "When a human breaks the branch with his hands, the tree knows the difference, and brings in substances to heal the wound."

Our boots crunch on through the glittering snow. From time to time, I think of objections to Wohlleben's anthropomorphic metaphors, but more often I sense my ignorance and blindness falling away. I had never really looked at trees before, or thought about life from their perspective. I had taken trees for granted, in a way that would never be possible again.

Wohlleben used to be a coldhearted butcher of trees and forests. His training dictated it. In forestry school, he was taught that trees needed to be thinned, that helicopter-spraying of pesticides and herbicides was essential, and that heavy machinery was the best logging equipment, even though it tears up soil and rips apart the mycorrhizae. For more than 20 years, he worked like this, in the belief that it was best for the forests he had loved since childhood.

He began to question the orthodoxies of his profession after visiting a few privately managed forests in Germany, which were not thinned, sprayed or logged by machine. "The trees were so much bigger and more plentiful," he says. "Very few trees needed to be felled to make a handsome profit and it was done using horses to minimize the impact."

He has been taken to task by some scientists, but his strongest denouncers are German commercial foresters, whose methods he calls into question. "They don't challenge my facts because I cite all my scientific sources," he says. "Instead, they say I'm 'esoteric', which is a very bad word in their culture. And they call me a 'tree-hugger', which is not true. I don't believe that trees respond to hugs."

Suzanne Simard (in a Vancouver forest) uses scientific tools to reveal a hidden reality of trees communicating with their kin. (Diàna Markosian).

At the University of British Columbia in Vancouver, Suzanne Simard and her grad students are making astonishing new discoveries about the sensitivity and interconnectedness of trees in the Pacific temperate rainforests of western North America. In the view of Simard, a professor of forest ecology, their research is exposing the limitations of the Western scientific method itself.

In the scientific community, she's best known for her extensive research into mycorrhizal networks, and her identification of hyperlinked 'hub trees', as she calls them in scientific papers, or 'mother trees', as she prefers in conversation. Peter Wohlleben has referred extensively to her research in his book.

Mother trees are the biggest, oldest trees in the forest with the most fungal connections. They're not necessarily female, but Simard sees them in a nurturing, supportive, maternal role. With their deep roots, they draw up water and make it available to shallow-rooted seedlings. They help neighboring trees by sending them nutrients, and when the neighbors are struggling, mother trees detect their distress signals and increase the flow of nutrients accordingly.

In the forest ecology laboratory on campus, graduate student Amanda Asay is studying kin recognition in Douglas firs. (Ecologist Brian Pickles at England's University of Reading was the lead author and collaborator with Asay and others on the project.) Using seedlings, Asay and fellow researchers have shown that related pairs of trees recognize the root tips of their kin, among the root tips of unrelated seedlings, and seem to favor them with carbon sent through the mycorrhizal networks. "We don't know how they do it," says Simard. "We just have no idea."

Another grad student, Allen Larocque, is isolating salmon nitrogen isotopes in fungal samples taken near Bella Bella, a remote island village off the central coast of British Columbia. His team is studying trees that grow near salmon streams. "Fortunately for us, salmon nitrogen has a very distinctive chemical signature and is easy to track," he says. "We know that bears sit under trees and eat salmon, and leave the carcasses there. What we're finding is that trees are absorbing salmon nitrogen, and then sharing it with each other through the network. It's an interlinked system: fish-forest-fungi."

Scientists are only just beginning to learn the language of trees, in Larocque's view. "We don't know what they're saying with pheromones most of the time. We don't know how they communicate within their own bodies. They don't have nervous systems, but they can still feel what's going on, and experience something analogous to pain. When a tree is cut, it sends electrical signals like wounded human tissue."

She points to a massive, cloud-piercing giant with long, loose strips of grayish bark. "That red cedar is probably 1,000 years old," she says. "It's mother tree to the other cedars here and it's linked to the maples too. Cedar and maple are on one network, hemlock and Douglas fir on another."

Why do trees share resources and form alliances with trees of other species? Doesn't the law of natural selection suggest they should be competing? "Actually, it doesn't make evolutionary sense for trees to behave like resource-grabbing individualists," she says. "They live longest and reproduce most often in a healthy stable forest. That's why they've evolved to help their neighbors."

Looking up at these ancient giants with their joined-together crowns, it's extraordinary to contemplate everything they must have endured and survived together over the centuries. Lethal threats arrive in many forms: windstorms, ice storms, lightning strikes, wildfires, droughts, floods, a host of constantly evolving diseases, swarms of voracious insects and now humanity.

Tender young seedlings are easily consumed by browsing mammals. Hostile fungi are a constant menace, waiting to exploit a wound, or a weakness, and begin devouring a tree's flesh. Simard's research indicates that mother trees are a vital defense against many of these threats; when the biggest, oldest trees are cut down in a forest, the survival rate of younger trees is substantially diminished.

Unable to move away from danger, falling in catastrophic numbers to the human demand for land and lumber, forest trees also face the threat of accelerating climate catastrophe.

Does Wohlleben think trees possess a form of consciousness? British scientist Richard Fortey, "I don't think trees have a conscious life, but we don't know," he says. "We must at least talk about the rights of trees. We must manage our forests sustainably and respectfully, and allow some trees to grow old with dignity, and to die a natural death." In rejecting the confines of the careful, technical language of science, he has succeeded more than anyone in conveying the lives of these mysterious gigantic beings, and in becoming their spokesman.

When told about Fortey's criticism, that he describes trees as if they possess consciousness and emotions, Wohlleben smiles. "Scientists insist on language that is purged of all emotion," he says. "To me, this is inhuman, because we are emotional beings, and for most people, scientific language is extremely boring to read. The wonderful research about giraffes and acacia trees, for example, was done many years ago, but it was written in such dry, technical language that most people never heard about it."

Forest networks feed rain systems, each tree releasing tens of thousands of gallons of water into the air annually. Diàna Markosian.

Article by Richard Grant March 2018

I propose that we know very little about our true nature and the world that and the life and the organisms that

127

surround us. We are totally unconscious and unaware of how important each life link is to the survival of the whole.

I had a dream it was by and large a dream that I found to be coming to the realization that there is a thread of consciousness throughout the universe and all living things on this planet. The planet is virtually alive. But if we open our minds to the infinite possibilities of realities if we release ourselves from the chains of our past whatever those teachings may have been, we come to a new realization that all life is interconnected. The world is one yet we treat it as if it is our garbage dump, we kill trees and animals for our own pleasure. It is a moral indignity and insanity.

This thread of consciousness extends to all living things from the basic life structures to the higher creatures on this planet.

Chapter 9
Universal Thread of Consciousness

This is by no means a scientific study but came as a deep realization of how everything is so deeply intertwined. It came in a subconscious dream one evening.

Flowers and plants all will point their leaves toward the sun to absorb the rays of the sun. The smallest of creatures like ants and bees communicate to each other where the food is by touching antennas and doing dances that will tell the others where to find the food. Some animals walk hundreds of miles to find water. Elephants will mourn their dead. Is all this not a type of consciousness? Consciousness is universal. It is much more than we think it is. We are not the only ones with this capacity. We only believe we have a higher level of functionality. How little we are in the scheme of things. How little we truly know and understand of the world we live in and ourselves.

By looking at just a random sampling of creatures and plants, we are all building blocks that came from random biological structures that gave way to a massive array of plants and animals. They all have different levels of communication and feelings; with a need to survive we are all the same. To think humans are so much superior to all is a fallacy that must be overcome if we are to re-think our existence and to re-integrate our species with the different lives that exist on this planet. If we do not, the planet will treat us like the virus we are, and will start over without us.

Virus—They are only able to reproduce by hijacking a host cell and using its machinery to build more copies of the virus. Nevertheless, new research from Israel's Weizmann Institute of Science indicates that even viruses can communicate with one another.

Proteins play a crucial role in helping cells communicate with each other. Teneurins sit on the surface of cells and bind to other proteins on the surface of other cells. Apr 19, RNA/DNA There are two main functions of RNA. It assists DNA by serving as a messenger to relay the proper genetic information to countless numbers of ribosomes in your body, with ribosomes being the small protein-creating factories located inside of a cell.

Single cells organisms, all single-celled organisms contain everything they need to survive within their one cell. These cells are able to get energy from complex molecules, to move, and to sense their environment. The ability to perform these and other functions is part of their organization.

Plants communicate through their roots by secreting tiny amounts of special chemicals into the soil all through the plant's root zone—what scientists call the rhizosphere. These chemicals, called root exudates, send signals to every other living thing in the root zone.

VENUS FLY TRAPS although it lacks a brain, the carnivorous plant Dionaea muscipula has a functional short-term memory system. Researchers working in plant biology found that not only does the plant better known as the Venus flytrap know when an insect lands inside a leaf, but it can also 'remember' when it arrived.

TREES—interact with each other and their environment and share resources right under our feet, using a fungal network nicknamed the Wood Wide Web. Some plants use the system to support their offspring.

ANTS—Scientists have known for decades that ants use a variety of small chemicals known as pheromones to communicate. Perhaps the most classic example is the trail of pheromones the insects place as they walk. Those behind them follow this trail, leading to long lines of ants marching one by one. Ants are highly social creatures.

BEES—How does a honey bee tell other bees when she finds the locations of rewarding flowers, a drinking hole, or even a great new home? She will fly home and dance. That's right, dance. Experienced bees use the angle of their body relative to the hive ceiling to tell others the direction and approximate distance of whatever they are dancing for. Yet honey bees can recognize faces, communicate the location and quality of food sources to their community via the waggle dance, and navigate complex mazes with the help of cues they store in short-term memory. Bees have collective decision-making skills; this 'wisdom of the crowd' phenomenon has been studied during swarming, when a queen and thousands of her workers split off from the main colony and chooses a new hive.

CLAMS—While the clams might not have made a 'conscious' decision in the way we do as thinking creatures, they were able to place their individual risk in context and vary their response. This ability to tailor a response to different risk levels is a sign of surprisingly complex neurology at work.

FISH—The undersea world isn't as quiet as we thought, according to a New Zealand researcher who found fish can 'talk' to each other. Fish communicate with noises including grunts, chirps and pops, University of Auckland marine scientist Shahriman Ghazali has discovered according to reports.

CRABS—A species of crab can learn to navigate a maze and still remember it up to two weeks later. The discovery demonstrates that crustaceans, which include crabs, lobsters and shrimp, have the cognitive capacity for complex learning, even though they have much smaller brains than many other animals.

WHALES—That all cetaceans can communicate with each other is amazing, but the communication between individuals in the same species is even more complex. Orcas 'speak' with a number of different 'dialects' and 'languages'…Bottlenose dolphins and Sperm whales from different parts of the world also have different dialects.

Dolphins—Research by scientists shows that dolphins do indeed communicate with each other using a wide range of sounds and gestures.

FROGS—Frogs have sophisticated nervous systems that allow them to use their senses and respond to their environment. For frogs, their main feelings center on safety, fear, and pain.

ELEPHANTS—Elephants, the largest land animals on the planet, are among the most exuberantly expressive of creatures. Joy, anger, grief, compassion, love; the finest emotions reside within these hulking masses. Through years of research, scientists have found that elephants are capable of complex thought and deep feeling.

MONKEES—Kanzi, a bonobo, is believed to understand more human language than any other non-human animal in the world.

APES—It is now generally accepted that apes can learn to sign and are able to communicate with humans.

HUMANS—Cells are the basic building blocks of all living things. The human body is composed of trillions of cells. They provide structure for the body, take in nutrients from food, convert those nutrients into energy, and carry out specialized functions.

All data above taken from Wikipedia.

How little we know. If this very little sampling of the life that surrounds us, creatures of all types and kinds that have feelings, that can communicate in their own ways, that feel pain, that react to dangers yet we treat animals like slaves for our own consumption. We are part of all that is living on this planet we are all interconnected but are totally **unconscious** of our reality. Our own bodies are made of trillions of living cells, what are other creatures made of...Cells!

"I realized that Eastern thought had somewhat more compassion for all living things. Man was a form of life that in another reincarnation might possibly be a horsefly or a bird of paradise or a deer. So a man of such faith, looking at animals, might be looking at an old friend or ancestors.

In the East the wilderness has no evil connotation; it is thought of as an expression of the unity and harmony of the universe. " William O Douglas, Go East Young man 1974.

Human Behavior toward Animals Hasn't Caught Up to the Science By Jessica Pierce and Marc Bekoff. (article below)

These days, daily newsfeeds are cram-packed with headlines representing the latest revelations into who animals really are. Chimpanzees rely on their close friends to help them relax. Pigs have something that sure looks like personalities. Elephants mourn their dead; so do whales. Even to a casual reader of headlines like these, it should be abundantly clear that, much like humans, animals have rich inner lives.

Since the 1960s, we've seen massive growth in the scientific understanding of what animals think, know, and feel; with that sea change in knowledge, we might expect also to see a profound shift in ethical attitudes toward animals. And yet, we argue in our new book, *The Animals' Agenda*, human behavior toward animals is increasingly out of sync.

But it's not enough. For many people working in animal advocacy, the failure to produce better ethical results has been a bitter disappointment. Optimism has given way to frustration, even alarm, about what is happening to animals globally. Animals are, by many measures, objectively worse off than ever before. Despite the extensive database on the cognitive and emotional capacities of cows and pigs, burgers and bacon continue to be popular foods. According to a recent report by the Worldwatch Institute, global meat

134

production and consumption have increased steadily over the past four decades, rising by 20 percent in the last decade alone. (See Meat page 51).

Part of the problem is that some of the regulations we currently have in place are illogical. Consider the 2013 Federal Animal Welfare Act and Regulations 'Blue Book' published by the USDA, which holds that rats and mice are not animals. This, despite the research showing that both species display empathy and experience a host of positive emotions: Rats laugh and like to be tickled, and mice can read pain in the face of other mice.

Much of the research into animal cognition and emotions neatly blends industry needs with so-called 'welfare' improvements. Simply put, the appeal to 'animal welfare' has become a form of moral justification for continuing human exploitation of animals. The basic premise of 'welfare' is this: "We're doing the best we can for the animals but we have to use them for human benefits."

The loss of freedom in animals also manifests in observable behaviors. Captive animals often display abnormal behavior patterns, such as polar bears endlessly pacing back and forth in a zoo enclosure, rats chiseling down their teeth by obsessively biting the bars of their laboratory cage, and pet parrots plucking out their own feathers. These animals are telling us in no uncertain terms that the conditions in which they live are driving them mad.

As we write in the book, animals want to be able 'to mingle socially, roam about, eat, drink, sleep, pee, poop, have sex, make choices, play, relax, and get away from us'. They want to live in peace and safety, just like we do.

In *The Animals' Agenda*, we offer a new paradigm we call the science of animal well-being, in which the life of every individual animal matters, and which commits to radically improved freedoms for animals, especially freedom from human captivity and exploitation. This means phasing animals and animal products out of meal plans. It means putting an end to captive breeding in land and water zoos and halting the practice of shipping animals here and there as breeding machines. It means phasing out the use of animals in biomedical and other invasive research. And it also means, on the part of potential consumers of exotic pets, a broad-minded consideration of what captivity means for these animals.

Not only must we seriously address sources of human-induced suffering, but we must also work to create a world in which animals are free to live their own lives and make their own choices. After all, humans aren't the only intelligent beings on Earth. (Jessica Pierce and Marc Bekoff)

"The universe is alive with consciousness, our planet is alive. Consciousness is lived reality. It is the feeling of life itself."

Given the similarities at the behavioral, physiological, anatomical, developmental, and genetic levels between *Homo sapiens* and other animals, we all experience the sounds and sights, the pains and pleasures of life. All of us strive to eat and drink, to procreate, to avoid injury and death; we bask in the sun's warming rays, we seek the company of our own, we fear predators, we sleep, and we dream.

Plants and animals are living their own consciousness, yet we deny them their due being. Every creature is here for a reason. Humans try to say this is good and this is bad. There is no good or bad there just is. We want to manipulate everything. We are undoing the very essence of creation. We want to be the creators, but in doing so we only create our own demise. We must be able to see this. Consciousness is not about mental alertness. You exist because you are, you know that you exist only because you are conscious, and so does every other creature, plant organism, all have different levels of awareness.

"We are the Inhumanity of a brutal intelligent and unconscious barbarian that cannot live without warfare among its own species. How can we understand the awe of our planet if we cannot even reconcile our own attachment to the very source of our existence?" – MA

Chapter 10
Move from Production and Consumption to Conscious Behavior

What are you following? What is your goal?

Is your goal to accumulate wealth and material things; that, unfortunately is not the goal to happiness. We are following the wrong path; our intelligence has led us away from our beginning of humanity. Our path continues to lead to the devastation of nature. Our intelligence has become our nemesis. If you can ignore all the advertisements that sell, sell, sell, you are half way there.

We as humans believe to have more material possessions is the secret to happiness. Unfortunately, that is the truth as broadcast by corporations for you to buy more for them to make more profits. We produce a huge amount of completely unnecessary waste. Companies are made to sell products that break down quickly and we need to buy more all the time. "This allows them to make more and produce more. Have you noticed products are not as reliable as they use to be and they do not last as long? Why? So they can become obsolete so they can make more. Why can we no longer find spare parts, so they need to be replaced? Why is it cheaper to buy a product than to fix it? All designed to sell more. Where do these products end up—in landfill why are they not re-cycled? Why do we not create laws to mandate product continuance? We need to legislate against planned obsolescence, fridges, washing machines, need to last 50 years instead of 10. They must be able to support the products they make for 50 years and must recycle their end of life products, not just dumped into nature.

Have you noticed you are paying more and getting less, smaller packages, or less product within the package, yet we are paying the same? Is it not false advertising? Yet we continue without a peep from governing officials.

Are you happier? No! When are you the happiest, when you are in nature, where do we go? Not in the city where you live. We go to the country by the river, in the forest, on top of mountains, near the sea and the oceans. Why? Unconsciously we want to be closer to nature because we are a part of nature.

Who are we? Our sense of happiness is only when everyone else is less than you. What kind of life is that? To want more than another person 'to keep up with the Joneses' Why? This just leads to more material consumption. What kind of life is that? Why have we constructed our lives like this? If the whole world is trying to accumulate more things we are in deep trouble. Why? Does one person need all these things? We cannot take them with us at the end, when we die. If you die, no one wants most of it anyway. Why does this have to be, to have more than everybody else? Have we lived life or have we worked to the bone to accumulate things that we do not really need?

Imagine if this happened to other creatures and animals, if all of them suddenly decided to take more than what they need what kind of planet would we have? If lions started to kill other creatures just to accumulate food or trophies, they would soon run out of their food source. That is exactly what humanity is doing. We unfortunately are the only intelligent and unconscious creature on the planet that behaves this way, to the detriment of ourselves and every other creature, with a disregard to all (plant, animal, water, soil, air.)

In order to sell their products, companies have put their best foot forward. Claiming their 'good' products whether it be chemicals, gas, coal, oil, endless products, as being good for you, (not so much for the environment). They dictate what is good what is bad, and we let them do it with impunity. Now they are greenwashing their commercials.

Can we change this behavior as humans? We can achieve a lot in terms of well-being, and building a healthy society. We need to be happy with what we have. We need to work and enjoy life more. However, we continuously work and spend money we do not have and are always striving for more. Spending our lives in shopping malls is that living?

This generation must act; must change, we are here now—global catastrophe is upon us! If we do not act the next generation will be way worse off than this one. People know what a mess we created with unbridled consumerism and our throw away products that are just bull dozed into nature, what an insane concept by intelligent creatures. We know what a mess we created unconsciously and cannot deal with it. Humans will struggle, our lives will be exposed us as to what kind of creatures we are, time will define us, but not in a good way. These are challenging times that confront us, that is when who we are what we are will define us in this moment in time. Are we part of the solution or are we the problem?

The problematic issues we have created over the last 200 years of industrialization. This is the time we all need to decide. Everyone needs to take a stand in these challenging times for humanity. Everyone must make this commitment.

We have no entitlement, nothing on this planet belongs to us, and we will leave it with nothing, like the pharaohs inside the pyramids. The planet and nature owe us nothing yet we owe it everything. To allow us to be here to be alive to breathe air, to drink water, to partake of what is earth's bounty that we are destroying.

Humans do not understand their nature. The only people close to understanding what life was about are the natives in every country who lived off the land, taking only what nature provided and only taking what was necessary for survival. Belly full, we are happy we live life. **They are not working,** nature continues to produce with abundance, and they took only what they needed. But now we take everything and leave nothing. We have cursed ourselves. "Civilized" societies went into the jungles and told the natives they are poor. We will enrich your lives with material things that you will need to buy and educate you to learn modern civilization. You will need to work to buy things. Ask your-self who was poor or were they enjoying life to the fullest without destroying everything around them? Yet we go into the Amazon and destroy their environment, how do we allow this to happen?

"We are all half alive. We are torturing ourselves on medications, getting high on chemicals of all sorts if we continue the next generation will be less than us. The next generation must be one step ahead of the previous generation to be able to wrestle with the fundamental problems this generation has created. If we produce a generation that is less than this one, we will not be able to evolve our *consciousness* on this planet." Sadhguru.

We can no longer think in terms of my nation, we must think in terms of the good of the whole planet of all of humanity.

"We shall continue to have a worsening ecologic crisis until we reject the Christian axiom that nature has no reason for existence save to serve man." – White Jr. The Historical Roots of Our Ecological Crisis 1967.

Chapter 11
Conscious Awakening

From this point on, human evolution is at a crossroad to either evolve or become extinct. It has to be a conscious evolution. If we do not become conscious, there will be no further progress from humanity. Monkeys and Apes (if they are still around) will advance man will not. We can only advance consciously. Somewhere nature trusted us, trusted our intelligence; nature believed that this species could be entrusted to take care of this planet and all of its creatures and plants and water we were given *'Noah's Ark'*. That humans would choose the path of living and nurturing each other and nature, not destroying nature and each other for only the benefit of the few. We have been trying to outsmart nature and ourselves to our own peril. We are seeking wealth but at what cost? Can we not see within ourselves the truth, do we not comprehend the immensity of our position on this planet? We, all of humanity need transform our lives from unconscious behaviors to *conscious* behaviors.

Just because everyone tries to be like everyone else does not make it right. Just because the majority rules, does not make it the right thing. Why does what the majority say become the truth? The planet, nature does not behave this way. Majority rules is not how nature works, it is a foreign concept in nature. We you and I all came from nature, we are all the same. What is is, what is not is not, if we work with life with nature, we can become connected to nature, as we all have become disconnected into an imagined human self-created reality totally disconnected from nature and our planet.

"Enlightenment" is what humanity needs now. Seek the truth; make friends with the truth, because those that find the truth will free themselves from the bond of enslavement of what the boundaries of society has outlined as what our lives should be. A life time of work or a path of awareness, the choice is yours. If you choose the life of work, your life is done. We require creating a sense of inquiry to the world we live in. Humanity needs to establish above all else that this planet and all of its wondrous nature as the only value that must be above all else.

We must within ourselves know that we can live life beyond profit; we can no longer live with the expectation of profit.

We are at the point where we consciously need to change how we interact with the planet and nature and ourselves. Shall we continue on this path? Or do we change our intelligence to one of conscious realization of our predicament. Our conscious response will give humanity a better chance of survival, rather than continuing on a path of self-intelligent annihilation. We have a conscious intelligence to determine what is right and what is wrong in life. The question is can we elevate our intelligence to the level of consciousness required?

The oceans where life originated is the canary in the mine, it is sending us a message of what is happening to our planet. Carbon Dioxide which is pumped in the air through cars, coal, industrialization, farming, this carbon dioxide returns to the oceans and is absorbed by the oceans. Carbon dioxide reacts with the water and creates acids that destroy corals that fish require as a habitat. It also warms the oceans and this warming if it continues; the life in the oceans will no longer be able to survive. An empty ocean devoid of life, is what we mankind are creating. The chemistry of the ocean is changing 10 times faster than in the last 50 million years. Since the beginning of the industrial revolution humanity has released 1 quadrillion pounds of carbon dioxide into the atmosphere and the oceans have become 30% more acidic. It is killing animals with shells and skeletons like coral reefs. The coral reefs have been here longer than any animal. *"It is the canary in the mine."* We are destroying the eco system in the ocean. Coral reefs have so much bio diversity of all the ocean life tied to them, this is a crime, yet we let it happen because we do not see the cause and effect in front of us. If we continue to pump CO_2 in the atmosphere at the current rate, we will lose all coral reefs by 2050. We will have crossed the threshold of no return. Plankton essential to all life in the ocean will die off due to warming oceans and acidification caused by CO_2 returning to and being absorbed by the oceans. (Ref: carbon dioxide and coral reefs www.globalwarming.com.)

"What we do not see is out of our mind and our consciousness." All the problems we are facing is really under our control, my country, religion, language, race, color, and above all these are manmade problems. Human

beings have created self-identities we all identify with certain things. We have in the self-identification we have forgotten the big picture; we have lost sight of the forest while cutting down the tree, we look up and the forest is gone. We are human beings first and foremost. We identify with all kinds of things to make us look different, but we are one. We identify with everything except the one key to our existence the care and welfare of this planet. We must change from a narrow sense of identity (I) (Me) to a larger global identity. A conscious sense of being must take place. Intelligence is in the human mind, but we are all unconscious of our own prejudices and our striving for comfort is destroying the very planet that has given birth to mankind. These limited identifications that humans have created are preventing us from becoming higher conscious beings. Once a false identity is created all of who we are; our emotions our intelligence our capabilities, everything is then focused on that established identity, to the detriment of the whole.

Has our current life situation worked? Or are we going to be another failed civilization? A large scale rising of human consciousness must happen. If not, our lives as we know it will go for generations suffering the decisions we make at this time now. Can we eliminate one problem which is me? Our children must create a new path of enlightenment, different from their ancestors who have destroyed nature to their own detriment and the detriment of generations to come. This is a lifelong mission. The solution is to develop social consciousness toward the planet and all humanity.

We have divided the world in the form of nations, religion, borders, race, creed, social status, political beliefs, and on and on. How many ways have generations of humanity divided itself to the detriment of all things conscious? We must have a goal to eliminate all divisions that prevent us from achieving planetary consciousness which then becomes a limitless identity. If we do not, populations will face mass die offs. A problem of this magnitude cannot be solved in a day. But we must start.

We are all one, we all came from the same beginning we are all human beings on one planet. We need the sense of oneness for the entire humanity. We need to achieve universal consciousness for and oneness for all of humanity. We must feel all people's suffering just as we feel our own. It is the realization that even our enemy is motivated by the quest for happiness and fulfillment. Reality teaches us that everything is interconnected. We can achieve a higher level of consciousness toward humanity and toward this planet and all the life it has created. If we want to live well, live well here, and enjoy life now and for generations to come. In our consciousness, we will realize that global economy equals global warming.

"The control man has secured over nature has far outrun his control over himself." The Life and work of Sigmund Freud 1953.

Conscious intelligence is an oxymoron. We are trying to shape our rudimentary knowledge of life into our intellect but we must shape our intellect into the knowledge of this life.

We project who we are with whatever identity we have attached to ourselves yet we are here without really knowing who we are. Yet, we are here projecting our wants and criticisms of all things that do not fall into our limited knowledge and intellect. We do this without even knowing who we are? Yet, we still fail to experience life.

Why do we think we are intelligent, and why are we not naturally enlightened? How conscious are we as human beings? Why are people unconscious? We have gotten trapped into our daily lives, driven by survival and an ever-growing ego and the materialism that feeds this ego. We have ourselves become too egotistical and are solely focused on improving me myself. Until this limitation is suppressed; we cannot achieve consciousness. We are caught in the wave of societal influences. Look at all the TV Ads, marketing influencing us to buy more and to spend more. In order to spend more, we need to work more and enjoy life less. This over consumption leads to the degradation of the beauty of nature, and a non-recognition of our own destruction of this very nature that is our life source. In the end, we will have less wild life, less water, less air, and in the end nature will say enough of this intelligent creature. As we continue along this merry path there is no way to be conscious of what is happening around us globally. It becomes self-defeating the whole world is not naturally enlightened, because we are too consumed about our own lives. How can we worry about other people in a faraway land let alone the animals the trees the water and the air.

As Carl Sagan would say in our solar system which is a tiny speck in the whole cosmos, in that solar system is a blue planet 'earth' a jewel among all planets and is even a smaller speck. In that tiny planet of a speck is your city, your town your village which is even a smaller speck. In all of this, we are big men and woman with giant egos. This is a serious problem, once we have created the illusion that man is great, we cannot be conscious we can only continue with our animalistic behaviors to consume everything (water, plants, animals, fish, air) and leave nothing for anyone or anything.

In trying to make our lives better, we have succeeded in depleting the planet of everything we need for our own survival. We have more comfort but less happiness, more toys, less birds, more trinkets less water, more cars less air, and more farms less trees, more chemicals less earth, more comfort less joy, more useless products and less enjoyment of basic life.

"When you defile the pleasant streams and the wild bird's abiding place, you massacre million dreams and cast your spittle in God's face." – John Drinkwater.

We are carnivorous animals at the top of the food chain with no consciousness of the food chain. With no consciousness on how it affects humanity as a whole. What other animal would fish the oceans until there is no fish left? Our intelligence has allowed us to deep freeze millions of tons of fish; while these fish are frozen, they are not reproducing. Can we not see? Are we that intelligent? How can we justify all of our insane behaviors? Do we not have a moral consciousness, or do we just say damn all the future generations because, that is what we are doing with everything. Do we catch the very last tuna to extinction?

Somewhere I read there are at minimum 200 species that become extinct every day.

What can I get here and now what can we get more than the next person. Imagine 20 billion people thinking the same way. There will be nothing left, again where is our consciousness, our intelligence.

How does one strive to have more mental alertness leading to consciousness? We can only be conscious when we stop being unconscious. Everything we do is at an unconscious level.

Is intelligence killing our planet? We give up our intelligence through fear. If we allow our intelligence to function, then all your beliefs will begin falling apart. Suddenly you know that you do not know. There will be a lot of social pressures to accept current norms and not to rock the boat. The billionaires do not like people rocking the boat. People will lose millions in the market place, as thousands of companies will close. The big losers will be the multi billionaires of those companies. It is a small price to pay for saving our planet.

We are too caught up in our daily time-consuming routines of work, sports, family, social activities, life just happens by chance. We know that we do not know. If you admit to yourself that 'I DO NOT KNOW', then you have to use your intelligence. Other-wise we are living in a psychiatric ward where only the doctors are lunatics. When you do not know, your intelligence becomes bright it is just a matter of thinking; is this right or is this wrong and not just accepting what we are told. When you say I know, then you no longer accept any other concepts or ideas. (Trump Syndrome) We as humans are not sincere enough to admit what I do not know. We do not understand the power of I do not know, only then can we seek the possibility of what it is I do not know. Everything we do not know we just assume until it is disproven by scientific evidence. When someone assumes something and gathers thousands of believers, there will be conflict. Why do we not just admit we do not know and avoid conflicts on this planet?

It is time we function intelligently as intelligent creatures on this planet. Can we transform the world are we committed to make it happen? Who are we? That is what we need to fix to get us in alignment with nature, to act as one to be a positive influence and energy. What do we want to be on this planet? We have all become many things that we are not. We are all the same.

We have enormous material needs, and this is not a simple problem. People suffer this for their whole life. Essentially, we as a creature on this planet have decided that we are the most important superior beings ruling this planet, what a fallacy. We cannot rule Mother Nature; it will treat us as another creature. We are just part of the entire web of life. But we are very quickly destroying our own existence because we cannot handle our own intelligence, we have become sheep. Your intelligence allows you to control your thoughts and your emotions and to think…really think about what is happening all around us. Should we continue to let it happen?

When are we going to learn to use our thoughts and emotions intelligently? If we do not use our intelligence, are we not handicapped? We need to use intelligence to get out of the mess we have created. Yet, we are stymied; we do not use our intelligence to sense that what is happening is totally wrong. Why let it continue? We are in essence destroying the future for mankind. Why has this happened? We have made unnatural divisions between countries and societies and religions that exist nowhere in nature except in human minds.

"Never look up to anybody, never look down on anyone or anything. If you see everything the way it is everything has immense importance, everything supports everything else." – Anon.

Every creature has value, but we as intelligent humans have only recently realized this. How many things on this planet have we destroyed and continue to do so. For what— The economy, really? We are destroying ourselves for the economy? Simply because we think this is valuable and this is not. There is nothing on this planet that is not important, life is all inter connected. We are just not able to see it, to see the large picture. We did not realize that every creature supports every other creature and to the quality of life of everything around us. Beavers building dams for habitat yet we only saw the fur and thought it to be a pest, how wrong we were. Yet we judge every creature this way. We want to be the top creature on the planet. If we continue, we will make this a horrible place to live as we continue to have that ideology, we will continue to destroy all that we need to live happy lives. If we treat creatures on the planet, this way we also continue to treat ourselves that same way. We divide ourselves even more.

We do it every day, day in and day out. To what end shall we continue this madness. We are creating misery for our future selves and yet we want to continue on this path. There is no fool like a human fool. People have such debt and investments; they must continue the same path of illogical world destruction. Humans want to have all their possessions and get even more of them. They are in a trap. We owe even more to the banks and we must work even more, and this will not lead to happiness.

We need to understand we may be giving all our energy to our lives right now. Time is passing us by, for all of us. We cannot undo time we cannot return to the past. What is ticking away is our lives. Time just moves on whether you are happy or unhappy, time does not care. Life and your life energy is passing you by and the true enjoyment of this life.

Fundamentally we are all looking for well-being. In the animal world when an animal is fed, it is content it will sit or sleep under a tree in the shade if humanity has not cut it down. What a simple life. What is the well-being of human being?

What is it? It is not what we think it is. It is quite different than what we think or is lead to believe. We are all connected; the planet is us and we need to evolve into an intelligent state of realization and consciousness about our reality. Evolution made us who we are, to take care of the planet and it will take care of us. Who destroys this planet the planet will in turn be destroyed. This planet evolved life over billions of years that manifests into a human form. We have pushed our own intelligence beyond reasonable bounds.

What do we have? We have intelligence, we have energy and we have limited time. This energy is in our hands. We hold the key to the use of our time. How we choose to live if we focus our energies to the wealth of Mother Nature instead of continuously impoverishing our own quality of life. If we take hold of this intelligence and use positive energy, we can make our lives on this planet so much better than what it is. Organize what we can organize and coming to terms with the realization that we need to change the way the human race is organized. This is where the equilibrium of life is.

People are uncompromising because of illogical beliefs. When one person believes something and someone else believes something else, then conflicts will arise. We convince people of these assumptions in our minds based on politics, religion, property, borders, language, and color whatever the difference we can find. Humanity has a long way to go. We may just destroy ourselves before we can evolve to a higher state of consciousness. We need to cross the great divide of consciousness of a sense of one; we are all the same no matter what our beliefs. We have made the 'soup' we live in and then we are surprised about the outcome. Why are we surprised?

People are constantly complaining the world should be a better place to live. Our communications are far superior to the past. We have communication on a global level. We can communicate to the entire world. Life spans are much longer; we have had no major wars for over fifty years, though tensions are always there due to ideological differences. The exception is Russia attacking Ukraine at the writing of this. Barbarianism is still within humanity. How can we instill consciousness across so many boundaries?

What is our next progression for this planet's consciousness? What is the significance of raising human consciousness? Consciousness is a dimension within us. It is not determined by the boundaries of our modest knowledge and memories and emotions. Our consciousness is a dimension of our intelligence beyond knowledge. Unless we all attain this dimension, we can talk about peace and unity as principles and values but, this will never resolve the human dilemma. We cannot see the planet as it is.

This is our time on the planet will our generation move forward to create a better place for future generations? It is time for us as humanity to decide. Are we going to seize the opportunity to make life better for all humanity or not? It is our decision here and now. Do we want to change? That is the question we our generation have in our hands the opportunity to continue humanity or not! That is the question. All we have is a little bit of time that is all we have; most people think they are immortal that is why we do nothing we think only other people die.

In 1945 after World War II, could you have ever imagined that all those countries would form a European union? It is a huge step in human consciousness. When people who fought this war could ever come together, it is a tremendous step for humanity, except for Great Britain who took a step backward.

We must focus on the here and now, to pay attention with your intelligence of what is happening on this planet today. Do not polluted rivers drying up deserve our attention instead of gazing at the stars? We spend billions going to the moon, while the planet is not being tended to.

By paying attention, we will realize that this planet is alive. If we are conscious, we become alive, we see, we feel, we vibrate, we energize, we become young again. What is time? Time is the clock to our lives; our lives are ticking away. We are trying to do many things, but not consciously.

Human intelligence has evolved over millions of years; our consciousness has yet to evolve. Should we not decide the destiny of our planet or should we let the planet decide our destiny? If we do not consciously take responsibility to enhance this planet to its former glory, we will become a footnote in history.

"A footnote to no one."

All other planetary creatures are in a natural instinctive nature. We are above all that, if we think we are here to help and not destroy then we become enlightened. Yet, we destroy all of the nature around us with impunity. The water, our life source, the air that we need to breathe, the soil that we need for our very survival, the earth we walk on, the oceans, plants and animals, nothing is safe from the ravages of humanity.

Most human beings are on a self-ego trip, not even realizing the harm we have created on this planet, our only planet, our only life, can we continue to slowly poison our own lives consciously; can we consciously destroy our rain forests, the lungs of the planet? Let us look ahead we cannot fix the past but we can change the future. We can create a better tomorrow through intelligence and a higher level of consciousness.

Human consciousness will become more valuable in finding our true path on this planet. We have to transform our intelligence to a higher level of social consciousness. The awareness of what is happening around us. A consciousness with intelligence can perceive what is right and what is wrong. A consciousness evolving to make nature our number **one priority** for our survival on this island a speck of dust called earth.

People need to perceive things as they are; not as they are presented to us, not as they are told by corporations, believe no one. Let your own consciousness be your guide toward your own intellect, we have become too swallowed up in day-to-day economic hysteria. We have lost our direction and cannot decide what is right and what is wrong, by putting profits and economic goals ahead of the welfare of this planet.

Consciousness—what is involved? We need to start with human planetary values. What are they? They are the false economic values, the lines have been blurred by industrialization. We need clarity to overcome the false goals we are all chasing. Everything you feel every action you take is due to our belief system that has been created by our predecessors. We are not even conscious of our own decisions and how those decisions affect us; affect our lives and the planet we live on. If we value or chase money (root of all evil), working for money is a very nice way to enslave you forever. If we value money more than happiness, our lives may be adorned with all kinds of material things, but there will be no fulfillment no inner peace. Our values are emotional levers that trigger our environmental response. If these values are at an unconscious level, we are on a path of self-environmental annihilation.

We therefore need to raise our mind to a conscious level of understanding of the long-term consequences of our actions. We need to reshape our core values that have been instilled by past teachings and beliefs. Information teaching is not intelligence, intelligence is developed from consciousness. Our information gathering has made us lose our way. We have lost our conscious interaction with the living planet. We all have the right values; we just need to synchronize them on a grand planetary scale.

Imagine how different our lives will be. What if we changed the value of money and replace it with the value of social and planetary consciousness. Changing our values consciously will change the direction of all our decisions. Our lives will increase in value as we become more in tune with our own consciousness and the environment around us. We need to tackle the more important things in life with health energy and vitality, with a youthful sense of wonderment and awe at the creativity of life. We all take life for granted, but it took billions of years for life to get at the point it is. Are we not in awe? Yet we destroy what is around us for what? money? That does not create happiness. There is more joy in living things and all that is around us. But we do not see.

Love of all things, we can experience love between ourselves, or the ultimate love of an animal the bond between a dog, a cat, a cow, a horse, it is all there for us to see and feel, even a tree. You need a higher level of consciousness, we all have it, and we just do not use it.

There is no greater power on earth than gratitude and appreciation of what we have. Gratitude automatically turns off any negative emotions that we may feel. It makes us feel good. It costs us nothing to practice gratitude every day, it makes us so rich. It takes nothing away from nature, but gives so much more power. How magical would our lives be if we all lived with a sense of gratitude? We have lost our kindness and compassion for fellow humans, for all creatures big and small, for nature. We must nurture our compassion toward all humanity and our whole environment. The world will be a better place if we showed compassion toward each other and nature. Ever see how good it feels when you are kind and compassionate toward another being, another creature. Do you notice how they respond; have you noticed a flower perk up to the sun or the sound of your voice or music? Have you noticed we are all interconnected in this web of atoms and molecules, have you? It feels good to be kind and compassionate because it is the right thing to do with all humanity and nature. Just think what our lives would be like if we were all compassionate to one another and nature.

Doing the right thing, we all know internally what is right and what is wrong. Yet, we continue to do the wrong things because it is easier and more convenient. We poison our rivers, yet we know it is wrong. Why do we continue? Why? The inner knowing, we must always do what is right, because it brings inner peace. That peace, what we are all striving for is the value of doing what is right. This is a powerful value. Are we doing the right things to nature? Are we? How would our lives be different?

We must be in conscious awareness to allow our actions to not be in conflict with those dimensions of natural law that keeps all life flourishing on this planet. We have been totally unconscious of our destructive behavior.

Where is our intelligence? Can we not open our eyes? Where is our consciousness? Are we so unconscious that we cannot see what is before us?

"Man has lost the capacity to foresee and forestall. He will end up by destroying the earth." Albert Schweitzer, quoted in James Brabazon.

But to do this we need enlightenment a consciousness of our understanding that we are all connected on this planet a living organism which contains life on this bio sphere.

We must evolve our consciousness into what really is our reality. This Planet! Until we realize we are all one we will not go forward. We must protect the biological nature of all that supports us, as a people of this planet. Not as you or I or me but of us all of us.

We must re-think all of our beliefs, to a new and higher consciousness of what we are doing to everything around us. We must evolve into a **'Consciousness of Awareness'**.

We have the evidence that we need to change. Piles of money will not make us happy; material things will not make us happy. When we die, we can't even take it with us. If we have no nature, no water, no air to breathe of what value is money? No value at all! We must evolve into a new understanding of our relationship with this living planet. Do we really want it to become a dead planet like Mars? We must evolve into a higher-level consciousness, to perceive what is true and reject what is false.

We must take inventory of our own prejudices, upbringing, faith, politics, and speak out against all that is not right with this planet. We need to step out of the box that prevents us from moving forward. The decisions our lives take on this our planet will affect our lives and all generations that follow us.

Our own biases thinking we know more than we do prevent us from moving forward, we ceased to question everything. We have the evidence before us. It is our unconsciousness preventing us to see. Only by developing a higher level of consciousness can we evolve to the next level of our evolution. Will we continue on our current path of self-destruction or will we change our ways. Why destroy the planet while we are here? Humanity does have an internal sense of right and wrong why have we stopped using it?

We are at the cross roads, we need no we must change our economic model to a planetary world model of '*Planetaryism*'.

"*We shall require a substantially new manner of thinking if mankind is to survive.*" – Albert Einstein.

Let's make that happen.

Chapter 12
Conscious Evolution

A single cell amoeba to a human being, billions of years of evolution. Human beings are at the peak of evolution. We have the highest level of intelligence and cerebral capacity. We are in a space and time where our evolution must be conscious. It is the next stage in our evolutionary development. We have the where with all capacity for humanity to transform itself for the benefit of all populations and the whole of the planet we live on and the natural environments that surround us. We are becoming aware of the significant role we play on this planet. We must grow this awareness to a consciousness that will allow this planet to grow along with humanity.

We live with the memories of things that are taught to us from generations. This determines what we will and will not do. Unfortunately, the discipline of consciousness has not yet evolved. We are relying on our memories of the past. Our own minds will turn against us. We still suffer what occurred yesterday, 20 maybe 100 years ago. What may happen in the future we suffer, before it even occurs. We need to talk about a '*conscious transformation*'.

We cannot transform ourselves into conscious beings unless we talk about the past. The past is what is holding all of humanity back, preventing us from transforming our lives on this planet. The attachment the security blanket of the past prevents us from moving forward.

War and peace, as long as humanity has had war, struggling with each other's human made ideologies, I am correct you are wrong we have struggled we have fought wars to force our beliefs unto others. As long as there was war, and we were fighting among ourselves the planet was safe. World War II lasted over 5 years; during those five years the oceans were able to increase the number of fish in the oceans. The population was limited because of the casualties of war. We are now faced with a new reality, that reality is peace but a new kind of peace, a peace with a self-realization that we are all one that we are all interconnected that we can only resolve our world issues by being one with each other.

World peace what a lovely concept, and now we have overpopulation. We achieve one goal then it all falls apart. We cannot just keep tackling one goal at a time. We need to change all areas that affect the livability on our planet, simultaneously. Are we committed to live on a thriving planet or a dead planet like mars? What are we committed to? We may have 10–20–30–50 years. We will go away and the planet has a billion years to rebuild itself without humanity.

Now we are in a space and time where our evolution must evolve from awareness to intelligence to consciousness. It is the next level in our evolution. Where we suddenly realize that we are all one all interconnected to this planet, what we do to this planet we do to ourselves. Once the planet's social behaviors awaken to this realization then we will have achieved social consciousness to ourselves to all other cultures, to all the life on this planet that is interconnected in a thin web supporting life. It is the next level in our evolution. When we look at the cosmos, our body may or may not evolve further but we must evolve consciously. The level of our intelligence must also evolve such that our experience with life and nature changes to become conscious of ourselves and of others and of all life that surrounds us. We must live within the bounds and limitations of our survivability on this our only world. We must evolve into a new conscious awareness of our interaction with nature and all life on this planet.

Our evolution must become conscious we can only progress consciously, if we do not from this point in time humanity cannot progress. Somewhere in time nature instilled intelligence into the human being. During this time we have been trying to beat nature to death with our intelligence. In the long term, this is impossible. Humanity is always craving for something more and more. We want wealth, possessions and more and more material things and as humans whatever we have is never enough. Can we not see within ourselves that this is not the path to happiness and self-fulfillment? Humanity has lost its way, its connection with the planet. We are living in direct opposition to the natural world that created us. We are not experiencing life we are working our lives like slaves never knowing why we do what we do to the detriment of ourselves and life around us.

Human consciousness should create our reality within nature. Right now; we are working against nature to our own detriment. We must support nature for our own survival. We must realize in this minute of our time, on a small planet in a huge universe. Unless we change consciously, our lives are going to have catastrophic consequences for future generations.

Consciousness enables us to see everything around us; we move forward from our darkness our mental handicap to enlightenment of consciousness. To do this we must create a conscious planet. We are intelligent but we need to evolve as conscious human beings to evolve on a conscious planet in a humanistic society for all. Consciousness and love for all beings all creatures and plants, air, soil, water everything we need to interact with ourselves and the survivability of our lives on this planet. *"The planet is alive we are alive, God will not help us we must help ourselves."*

Because we think we know everything, (Trump Syndrome) we have never paid close attention to every aspect of life around us, we simply ignore everything. Pay attention to the life happening around you, a worm an insect a bird. We continue to ignore all of the life that surrounds us. We need to pay attention to the life around us, and our lives within this planet. Are we going to get rid of all of it? The birds, the plants, the animals, the fish, the coral reefs, the trees, the rivers, the lakes the ocean, are we that intelligent? (Sarcasm) Pay attention to an ant or a bee, who says we are more intelligent than they are? These are some of the smallest of creatures yet have a very sophisticated social order. All creatures have some sort of consciousness and are more aware of their environment on this planet than

165

humans. Global warming is here and birds are already nesting a month earlier; they are already aware of what is happening. Bees and ants have a much more organized society than humanity. Who are we to say that a bee or an ant is a lowly creature. Who said we are the only most intelligent being walking on the planet? If we remove all the plants and creatures from this planet humans will not survive. However; the reverse is true, remove humans and the planet will flourish once again. <u>Remember this</u>!

Who told us we are the most significant life on this planet? The idea that the universe is human centric is an idea that was created by man. Remember when we believed the earth was the center of the universe everything revolved around us, the moon and stars and all the planets. That was also a religious belief. This was disproved by scientific evidence from Galileo. He was excommunicated by the Catholic Church for revealing this fact to the rest of humanity. In this part of the galaxy, our solar system is small. If tomorrow the entire solar system disappears, nobody will notice it. You see humanity is so big, with great material needs.

We will all return to dust one day back to the elements that created us, and we have not enjoyed life. We remain unfulfilled destroying everything in our path to what end?

If anyone says there is a better place than this planet in the cosmos and all its life and bio diversity, then why can we just not improve life here instead of trying to search for the unknown; the impossible? We are searching the heavens we should be fixing the planet. It is like the grass is greener on the other side of the fence. It has always been green; we just never took care of it. It is because we have not taken care of our own planet that we have destroyed so many things on this our only planet. There is no other planet, there is no heaven there is only here and now, if we do not take care of this planet here and now, there will be none for humanity tomorrow.

"We must be forced to explore the universe in search of a new home because we have made the earth inhospitable, even uninhabitable. For if we do not solve the environmental and related social problems that beset us on earth—pollution, toxic contamination, resource depletion, prejudice, poverty, hunger—those problems will surely accompany us to other worlds." Donald G. Kaufman and Cecilia M. Franz, Biosphere 2000—Protecting our Global Environment 1996.

People always want answers the logic to the questions, sometimes there are no answers. But our leaders in history did not want to say I do not know. (Trump Syndrome) That is where religion filled in a very nice niche. Why are we here? No one knew, maybe few asked the questions we just were. But humanity did not know. What we want is peace of mind and how to be happy here and now. Who created all this wondrous life it must be a super being, what else can it be? Going into ancient history there was the god of thunder, the god of the sun, the god that brought floods and ravages, draughts, on and on. All associated with an act of God. We now know this is caused by nature. Intelligence grew again these idols that were created are false idols. There is only one Supreme Being that created all known by many names in many cultures. Science has dispelled many religious beliefs. Intelligence is once again growing through scientific research that the path to humanity was not a straight path there were many divergent species that did not survive.

Our human intelligence evolved again, to understand that our very existence was created by every atom and cell that exists in all the plants and animals on this earth. All have some common biological material; we are all the same existence. We are all interconnected, at the smallest cellular levels. No one is different from each other we have evolved from earth matter and our intelligence has evolved. We need to reconnect with our past.

"A living planet is a much more complex metaphor for deity than just a bigger father with a bigger fist. If an omniscient, all-powerful Dad ignores your prayers it's taken personally. Hear only silence long enough, and you start wondering about His power, His fairness, and His very existence. But if a world mother doesn't reply, Her excuse is simple, She never claimed conceited omnipotence. She has countless others clinging to her apron strings, including a myriad of species unable to speak for themselves." – David Brin.

Why are we afraid to say I do not know? (Trump Syndrome). Meaning only exists in our memories we are constantly looking back into our memories. Past memories rule everyone's lives. So much so the past becomes our future. Memory in fact needs to be looked at with an inquisitive mind, and not to hang over us like Damocles sword. Our entire body is memory, genetic memory, memory that is conscious and unconscious. The whole body is memory not just the mind. If you are unhappy at your job, is it the mind that is unhappy or is it the billions of cells that are telling you the job you are doing which may be against nature telling your mind something is not right, the pay is great but I do not feel good. Why?

The body retains every bit of memory with its billions of cells. You need to use your whole body not just the brain. This is one of the differences between being fully or just partially conscious. The mind, this intelligence has education, religion, all your memories, political affiliations all your biases that do not allow you to use your body to a full conscious ability.

We need a '*Paradigm Shift*' In our lives on this planet. What we want is peace of mind, and how to be happy here and now. If something is fundamentally right, why are we afraid? We are born on this planet, everything else is taught to us and different cultures teach different things. We are told what to believe. It is time to release the chains of our past! We need to stop the teaching that makes us less than human beings. We must change our message to children. The world is burning up are we not concerned? Humans by nature are compulsive, we need to change our compulsive behaviors, and the only cure is consciousness. We need to change our compulsive behaviors to one of '*Planetary Consciousness*'. The well-being of our planet will lead to the well-being of all civilization. When will we learn the truth '*the planet is the source of our well-being*'. We as human beings need to put our lives in sync with the well-being of this planet.

How do we get to this point of consciousness? We are misunderstanding consciousness as mental alertness. Mental alertness will only help us to survive better in the wild. In nature, everything has its own level of consciousness. The question is how conscious are we?

What have we done to raise our level of consciousness? What have we done in our civilization? Our education system of three R's read, write, arithmetic has not evolved. We still teach one to be better than another. We are instilled with competitiveness the only goal is to be better than someone else. We have not taught our children the richness of this planet, the wonder of nature, to protect every living creation that ties all of the planet together.

"Our children may save us if they are taught to care properly for the planet; but if not, it may be back to the ice age or the caves from where we first emerged. Then we'll have to view the universe from a cold dark place. No more jet skis, nuclear weapons, plastic crap, broken phones, drugs, cars, waffle irons, or television. Come to think of it, that might not be a bad idea." – Jimmy Buffet, Mother earth News, Mar/Apr 1990.

Today is the most important time of our generation. That we this generation decides our next step of evolution on this planet. Animals do not decide what they want to be, they react to their internal instincts of survival. As humans we can decide what we want to be, we as an intelligent species, the total planet needs to decide what course of action we will take. Are we with the planet or are we against it? That is our choice, if we nurture the planet the way it has designed itself, we will exist for billions of years, if we continue on the path we are on, I do not want to be here on a desolate planet in 100 years. The most significant is this very point in time where we can decide our own conscious evolution toward ourselves and this planet.

You exist because you are. Yet, we are not paying attention to every aspect of life that surrounds us. When will children be taught the wonders of nature? We are taught many things, what we are not taught is that every living creature from plants to animals has various levels of conscious perception. Everything around us is alive with the ever changing and evolving beauty of nature. Everyone should be in awe of nature. Unfortunately, we are not we treat it as if it was there for us to do whatever we want, the hell with the consequences. Our intelligence is full of information that is taught at a young age. Therefore, we think we know everything. (Trump Syndrome) In fact, what we know may change the course of this planet's evolution for humanity.

What is unique about being human? Information is useful, but the intelligence of knowing that the planet has far more power than us. A billion years more power than 200 years of human industrialization. Intelligence will allow us to navigate thru any situation. We are faced with global warming what are we going to do, what I hear is we need to adapt to global warming. That is using our intelligence. To adapt means we do not change our behaviors we just continue on as we have and adapt our lives to the inevitable consequences of our planetary digressions. We must change our behaviors not adapt to the changes coming because they will continue bringing pain to humanity. We need to change our intelligence and awareness and move to a consciousness of us and the planet around us to live cohesively without destroying the planet that has created our intelligence. We are no longer paying attention to what is around us, we lose our ability to use our intelligence in a higher manner. We can all achieve this through a higher consciousness.

Why are we the way we are? We cannot fix yesterday, but we can create a better tomorrow. What we do on this planet will affect tomorrow forever. Do not let the planet we have created turn tomorrow into a 6th mass extinction. We have taken life's creativity and tried to make it fit our own life styles. Our image of cities built in concrete with asphalt and cement to cover nature's growth. Cities with cars and pollution and we have taken away the trees and the plants. All we have left is a jungle of metal iron and cement buildings. Is this what we want?

We must change our relationship with this planet that has evolved us into humanity, (the chosen one). The planet has evolved different creatures over billions of years; there have been catastrophic events that have wiped out creatures of all kind. Yet, nature has always re-assembled new life. If we as humanity do not get in sync with nature, it will end us. What we do at this point in time is entirely our choice. To continue on the same path of reckless industrialization or of a new path of evolution with nature, it is our own choice now, we must be made aware consciously of our interactions with this planet.

This is the point in time where human evolution must take its next step. We cannot continue on the path of planetary self-destruction. We must become conscious of the planet we have evolved on. This is the next evolutionary enlightenment for humanity. If we do not get this evolutionary development right, no one will be here to say mea culpa. We as humans can determine the next step in our evolution; unlike any other creature we can determine the outcome. This requires a total transformation, a paradigm shift of what we were to be and what we can be. We need to hasten our evolutionary process to become conscious of our environment to live with nature not against it. Nature will win every time. It has billions of years to play with we do not.

We have two choices continue as we are and do nothing or radically change. Radically changing will hurt many entrepreneurs who have taken this planet for granted. There can still be entrepreneurs but everything must be done to promote planet health.

We must be caretakers of this planet, if we take care of it will take care of us, because evolutionary changes happen gradually.

"It is imperative to maintain portions of the wilderness untouched so that a tree will rot where it falls, a waterfall will curve without generating electricity, a trumpeter swan may float on uncontaminated water—and moderns may at least see what their ancestors knew in their nerves and blood." – Bernard De Voto Fortune June 1947.

Chapter 13
Why Is the Problem
Not Resolved

Why can we not change easily? We as humans have our comfort zones, and we do not want to upset our comfort zones. When we are young, we are not looking for our comfort zones we are looking at enjoying life. When we grow older, we look for comfort to be undisturbed from our comfort zones. When we are young in our teens, you had wild dreams in life. Then when you reach 30 you changed. You want comfort you have become ingrained in the comfort of society. I am becoming practical, I need a job; earn a living, then at 40 if I don't get in any trouble that is enough. That is when we start getting into trouble. You are not looking at life; you're looking at creating a safety net. The more security oriented we are the more change will disturb us. It's human nature.

There is no easy answer, everything is interconnected and the problems are of a global nature. All the rivers, the oceans, the trees the plants the animals and ourselves are all interconnected we are all one. Until we come together as a species to tackle our insane behaviors on this planet as one, we will not progress very far. We need to change our behaviors from consumerism to environmental consciousness. Why does humanity deny we have a problem? We know what causes the problem and we do nothing on a tangible worldly basis. We choose the path of least resistance of least upheaval. Change is difficult particularly for a human species that agrees on nothing. But, if we are doing something wrong would it not benefit humanity to do something radically different, like trusting one another. Trust that we can all work toward the well-being of the planet.

Everything is interconnected if you haven't already figured it out. Overpopulation, and consumerism drives the need for more industrialization, more energy, more extinction of species, more automobiles, more gas, more pollution, more forest destruction, more global warming, more plastics, more overfishing, warmer oceans, more farming, more chemicals, more fertilizers, more polluted rivers more ocean dead zones, more household and government debt driving even worse decisions.

In our drive to industrialization and consumerism, we have created a monster, the need for energy. The need to consume higher energy will lead to continued environmental disasters. The true cause of global warming and disregard for the environment is our thoughtless attitude toward nature. In our technologically and scientifically minded world, we seem to have forgotten that mankind is only a relatively minor part of nature that is causing damage far beyond what is acceptable. We believe to be able to control nature instead of trying to arrange ourselves with nature. This is the true main cause of global warming.

Although we are only guests on earth, we behave as if no further guests will arrive after us. Someone who respects nature and regards mankind as a part of a larger whole would never dream about using up nonrenewable resources in a short time nor would they contaminate the environment with huge amounts of pollution. Preservation of nature is not given a high priority. Shall economic growth and an ever-increasing personal income continue to be the reason for being here, in this life, beyond everything else?

Our lack of understanding has thrown life on earth, and the planet itself to be threatened. Money driven corruption drives governments and corporations. Who think they have a right to take or do anything they want on this planet.

Greed, money, power corruption will destroy this planet. The Power of 8 Christine Delory Nov 2010 (Below).

Money, business, competition, and the incorporation of anything that is useful is believed to be the principal means of gaining personal; power in the world.

Knowledge is power. But when knowledge is manipulated in order to gain power, true understanding of the realms of destruction is lost. Money is power sprang from this shortsighted point of view. Our lack of understanding has thrown life on earth, and the planet itself, so far out balance that the continuance of life as we know it is seriously threatened. The money-driven corruption drives governments, politics, and big business. While greed fights on for what it believes is its right to take everything.

By its nature, greed ignores any reality that does not feed its hunger for more. Greed must also convince others to deny reality so that its power-seeking mission can continue unobstructed. Greed must control, manipulate the truth, and capitalize on anything that suits its purpose, even if it stands to destroy life.

Power-hungry people distort the truth by making it appear that they have more power than they actually have, using the natural emotion of fear as a weapon from which to overpower. Denial of reality has been the main cause of the great imbalance we are now waking up to on Earth, environmentally.

The imbalance is being perpetuated by those who stand to lose what they've got should the playing fields of life be more even, and by those who are still mistaking their denials for reality. Now, truth is breaking out all over the place, only to be denied again and again by those whose purposes are served by keeping the truth locked away.

Denial does one thing only. It denies. It even denies that it is denial, and that it is denying. We can now see this quite plainly in many people who hold powerful positions.

"We lie the loudest when we lie to ourselves." Eric Hoffer.

It is important to understand what denial is because it exists in all of us whether we deny it or not. *"Denial's mission is to capture the truth and stop it from reaching our consciousness"* **and realizing the importance of the destruction that is happening all around us.**

Truth then reaches consciousness in a roundabout way—through 'gut' feelings. Now, the truth is breaking out all over the place, only to be denied again and again by those whose purposes are served by keeping the truth locked away, why do we need whistle blowers and why are they punished for telling the truth?

Denial has taken such a hold on Earth that we have to bring ourselves to the edge of extinction in order to realize how ignorant and misinformed we have been about so many things.

The overall understanding of humanity is increasing now. A massive shift in consciousness is occurring, visibly and measurably, one individual at a time. This is personal—and if you're not denying, you can certainly feel the winds of change howling through the world right now.

But this time, change really does mean change—a completely new way of life that is almost impossible for people to imagine at this stage—a way of life that enables us to evolve out of denial, to face reality no matter how dreadful it happens to be, and find ways to reclaim our planet.

Truth is the only thing that can lead us out of our present circumstances.

Greed takes control, and greed is the opposite of satisfaction. It can never get enough—even when it appears to have it all—because it is afraid of losing what it already has! It needs to control everything. It tells us that we must do what it says or some terrible fate will befall us. It tells us that, in such a dangerous world, we have no rights at all. To have no rights is to be enslaved. In an atmosphere of greed, human rights violations are seen as a minor hiccup. The system is greed, and as far as greed is concerned, if such violations produce more money and power, then that should be the way of the world!

The weight of the truth is rising through the genuine desire for real and meaningful change, but until then our greed will destroy the planet. We can see that we will destroy ourselves if we do not make the right changes. There are many out there who would rather die than change but not only do they die but every generation after them also dies.

The environmental condition of earth is a huge reflection of just how dumbed down we've become.

How can any intelligent being suggest that now that the polar ice caps are melting, we should drill for oil in the most important and sensitive balance points on the planet, the ocean, and in the Arctic. Greed wants to drill into them in its relentless and mindless search for more oil. These are the same people that will drill for oil into the Amazon and destroy the lungs of the earth.

In her effort to survive, Mother Earth is begging us to stop what we're doing to her not because she will die, but because we will.

People are still denying these survival warnings. Inaccurate assessments and wrong diagnoses, misunderstandings, underhandedness, falsifying the truth, the manipulation of rules, winning at any cost, ruthlessness, bullying and, of course, denial, denial, denial.

Mighty corporations have billions of dollars to spend to throw legal blocks at every turn they are not part of the solution they are the problem. Everyone talks about being green only because they have been pressured to so but in reality, they are not green they are the problem.

We must help the process along by lifting ourselves out of our own denials, no matter how unfamiliar the concept feels, no matter how strange it sounds, and no matter how much emotion we have to let ourselves feel in the process.

People see some awful thing happening in the world and they ask, 'where is the outrage? Doesn't anybody care?' Consequently, nothing gets changed.

Look at the illusions that we mistook for life, and to look at reality head-on. The more we see things as they really are, the more emotional our lives are becoming, the more intelligence we gain, and the more determined we are to be honest with ourselves and each other about our problems, our blessings, and our potential to change the habits and patterns of generations. That is the key changing the habits of generations that has evolved into industrialization, economies that measure wealth through money with total disregard for the effects we as humanity are having on this planet. The only planet we will ever know.

We can produce an evolutionary movement away from the edge of self-destruction, when enough dots are connected. Article above on greed, by Christine Delorey.

"When we heal the earth, we heal ourselves." – David Orr.

Greed ignores reality, and convinces others to ignore reality; it manipulates the truth of the realities surrounding us. Denial has brought us to the edge of the abyss. Truth needs to reach our consciousness; the truth is, greed can never get enough. In a time of great greed, the environmental conditions on earth is a reflection of how numbed we have all become. But, don't you worry; the politicians and corporations have our backs. (Sarcasm).

"There is a sufficiency in the world for man's need but not for man's greed." – Mohandas K. Gandhi.

"WEB OF ENTANGLEMENT" What is the web of entanglement?

It starts with greed, and power corruption it is prevalent in every country, every industry, and every monopoly. We say America is the land of the Free. The fact is the big wealthy business owners control things and make all the important decisions that benefit themselves. Politicians are elected to protect we the people, it gives us the illusion that we have a free choice. You do not, you have no choice. Politicians are paid by the taxpayers and then paid by lobbyists for all kind of nice things and trips; they are hired as consultants and the board of directors of corporations to ensure that the profits of corporations are not dried up by the goals of the people for clean air, clean water, clean soil, and clean environment. Laws are not passed to enforce strong measures that are necessary to stop the rape and pillage of nature for profit. The owners of these large corporations and multi nationals own everything and have long since bought politicians, senators, congress, city halls. They own all the big media companies and control just about every piece of news and information you get to hear. They make more for themselves less for everyone else and the environment is dying around us.

They do not want the population of citizens to become capable of critical thinking. They do not want well informed citizens; that do not help them and their interests of greed and power. They tell you what to believe, what to think and what to buy. They don't care about you or the planet. Nobody seems to notice or seems to care. That is what they are counting on. We will remain ignorant and continue to lead our diminished lives forever working in debt in an ever-diminishing planet.

This is a search for truth, and we need to find the truth seekers among the world population. There may be 10–12% of us (environmentalists, scientists, truth seekers,) that are ahead of the curve that are enlightened to find the truth of how and why we are here. You must be unbiased and undaunted. You must question everything. Question everything leaders are saying. If you do that, you will find the truth. Ask the question why, 5 times to find the truth of why we are poisoning our own planet our own environment who are we benefiting, it is not the working individual. Because in reality if we had a rich planet and only took what we needed and shared with all people and all creatures, we would not be in the mess we are in. This is our heaven on earth, but we are treating it insanely and destroying our own existence. If we continue, it will become our hell.

Why has the problem not been resolved? Three answers our Web of Entanglement, Cognitive Incapacitation and Greed.

Chapter 14
Cognitive Incapacitation

We no longer see things the way they are. Our minds are full of misinformation that it no longer has any clarity as to what is really going on. We are blind to our reality. Global warming is warming the oceans, melting the polar ice, causing rising oceans that will cause catastrophic flooding on land. These oceanic upheavals will continue around the planet, leading to catastrophic weather patterns. We are blind to our reality. We must exercise intelligence and consciousness. Scientists have given us clarity but we lack consciousness. What is preventing us from moving forward? As thinking evolves then we will know we were wrong. Why wait? Why do we assert the wrong things? It is due to social pressures and misinformation. If we think we know everything, then we will continue on the path of self-destruction. Knowledge gives us information, but not awareness of consciousness. Do we need more planetary upheavals to find our consciousness?

The beginning starts with one self. The answer is always within us. How do I create a maximum impact in the world? How do I use my mind, my energy my intelligence consciously? We always think the world is unfair, and those that do not do well always complain. Whatever happened in life, because nature has no judgment it just does what is best for nature. Whatever happens, be it good or bad it is just part of nature. Nature does not care about you or I nature just is. It will continue to evolve as it always has, but humanity has willingly or unwillingly tipped the balance of what makes this a very unique planet that has created the most wonderful biodiversity that has taken billions of years. We in our selfish egotistical nature are turning back the clock. We are facing another mass extinction because we have poisoned our own existence.

We are the problem. If you avoid challenges, you will avoid all possibilities of life. It takes some intelligence to see what is wrong and then clarity and consciousness to overcome it.

Alcoholic Anonymous acknowledges that until a person admits that they are alcoholic, the problem cannot be fixed. We are all walking on this planet in a state of alcoholism not even recognizing we have a serious problem. In order to fix this problem, we need to fix ourselves that is the starting point to recognize 'Houston we have a problem'.

Human beings have lost contact with reality. No one has really understood where we all came from. The planet has been here for over 4 billion years. Humans at some form or other have been around for 200,000 years. Humans with some knowledge and spiritual belief have been around for some 2,000 years. Humans using intelligence to create mass industrialization have been around for the last 200 years. The next 10–20 years will be the most important years in our evolution as a species on this planet. The choices we make now will determine our future.

The nature of life is still a mystery. How and why do we exist? Humans need to find an answer as to why. Humans to answer this question have created many religions to fill the need for knowing. We can become life and know life; however, we cannot completely understand the mechanism that nature uses to produce a myriad of life. If we decide to be a part of life instead of against it, we will recognize life for what it is. The only way to know life is to be integrated in life. Life is an ever-grand selection of diverse billions of possibilities. Once life has a chance to propagate; it just explodes into millions of outcomes. This boggles the human mind. We are not experiencing life. We are just a jumble of memories, thoughts, ideas, emotions, opinions, and a multitude of prejudices. These things are dominating our lives and not allowing us to just enjoy the beauty of nature, to be in awe of nature. We are not experiencing the life that we are in the mystery that is life.

We no longer see things the way they are. Our minds are full of misinformation that has no clarity as to what is really going on. We are blind to our reality. Awareness in combination with intelligence and unbiased knowledge, are the ingredients required to exercise consciousness. What may be true now may not be true 10–50 years from now as our understanding evolves. What was true 100 years ago is no longer true yet we hang on to the past and cannot let go. Thinking evolves, and then we will know we were wrong, but why wait? Why do we assert forcefully the wrong things? Why do the police remove logging protestors? Who is right and who is wrong? Why are the police not there to protect our environment? Why do we protect companies that destroy the environment? Because they pay taxes that pay the government debt and the companies hire people who in turn pay taxes and buy more products for which we pay taxes. We are all caught in a vicious 'web of Entanglement' with our present world economic conditioning.

"In America today you can murder land for private profit. You can leave the corpse for all to see, and nobody calls the cops." Paul Brooks The Pursuit of Wilderness 1971.

The 'web of Entanglement' involves countries that are so far in debt there is no way to get out of debt, countries just print more money. The only way to get out of debt is to create and collect more taxes. Taxes come from producing more products (GDP) which requires more energy (Gas and Oil). This causes more pollution in CO_2 and other gases which causes global warming and the products that are produced are not recycled they are dumped back in nature to pollute the very water and earth we need to live. We are in a vicious cycle that governments cannot let go of. The fires are here, but we do nothing, we will be proactive and fight them with more manpower that is not the answer. We are attacking the symptoms and not eliminating the root cause of global warming.

This is why rents, housing costs, food costs the governments have no interest in capping the cost as they collect too much taxes for the debt for a debt they cannot repay. The economic web is insidious.

"It is horrifying that we have to fight our own government to save the environment." – Ansell Adams.

The current economic model needs to be thrown out. It is not working for the benefit of this planet or the humans that inhabit this planet. Why do we assert the wrong things; because of social pressures and misinformation. If we think we know everything (Trump Syndrome), then we will continue on the path of self-destruction. Have you ever talked to a religious fanatic; there is no other truth but their truth. Knowledge gives us information but not awareness. With the information of supposed knowledge, we are going our merry way unconsciously in life. We do not see anything with any kind of consciousness; we are unconscious to our reality. Our perceptions are cloudy our knowledge is biased, we have stopped to think. This unconsciousness makes us blunder through life not seeing any of the realities upon us. Thinking you are right and that I am wrong has forever shut our minds to any other ideas or thoughts. The most important aspect of life is not what is told or taught but what you see. What we see is important, not what someone tells you what you should see. We need to see the situation clearly as it exists. We need to bring un-ambiguity of thought to develop consciousness. Society, government, religion, corporations, leaders of all types who say they are right are all dulling our individual intelligence and reasoning. The only way to free ourselves from the chains thrown upon us is to become conscious of our reality on this planet.

There are so many roadblocks, but the major roadblock is humanities' self-inflicted scope of self-identity. We identify with our own kind. It makes us who we are and, in the process, we deny everything else. Why are these differences too wide a chasm to cross? Humanity made them up to separate us from each other. What are they you ask? I can describe it by one word: discrimination. Let me count the ways, skin color, language, culture, religion, political beliefs, anything that is foreign to us is to be discriminated against. Endless wars were fought defending these beliefs. If we could not defeat the perceived enemy, then our next step was assimilation.

After thousands of years where are we? We are right where we started yet with more information that we garnered over the centuries from one culture to the next. We built upon everyone's learning in the arts and sciences in architecture, and engineering and science. So we have learned to take the best of every culture. We have built a civilization with that last 50 years of peace, but we still hold all of our prejudices.

We still have planetary conflicts, such as China and Taiwan. Countries like Russia and the Ukraine. Israel and Lebanon, Iran and Iraq, and the list go on and on. There are big blocks of countries that fear other countries because of religious doctrines and political beliefs and historical injustices. Countries want more land, access to natural resources and the next war will be over water. We have not on this planet yet achieved a level of realization that finally says we are all on this planet together and what we do as species affect the planet and each other.

How can we achieve global consciousness if we cannot achieve global understanding and compassion and trust to one another as a species? This is a very big and real issue. Unfortunately, unless and until we get rid of our self-identities it may not even be possible even in a peaceful environment. We need a world disaster to put all of our heads together to solve a global problem. This global problem is upon us Global warming and the destruction of global life is upon us because of humanity and its industrial economic pollution. We are the only ones that can solve it together, not just one country but every country working in unison. Unless we all work together globally and forget our past, the continued outcome will be disastrous for humanity. We must forget the past and work toward a future or we will have none.

When we give of ourselves in time, not just money Karma always ensures what you give is given back. We give because that is our nature; we need to value giving more in our lives, giving back to others giving back to nature. Give back to nature and nature will provide, take away from nature you will have nothing left. Because we do not give back—Karma! Human beings are wired to grow, to learn, to question, to try and understand who, what, where, why, and the how of things. That is what makes us who we are. Growth comes from experience, from failures. We just need to acknowledge that we have reached the pinnacle of survival on this planet. That pinnacle is our failure to realize that our continued path of destruction of nature through pollution and global warming is the self-realization that we are utterly alone. When we suddenly realize we cannot live without the life providing nature around us. This does not mean we improve our life styles, it means getting better so we can give more to the world, to nature and the rest of humanity. We can experience more joy. When we give back, we enjoy the world so much more. Our problem is we have not given back, we take and then we take again. We need to identify what is truly possible and we can, if we gain a higher level of consciousness. To get us back to our roots, back in touch with nature. Nature can bounce back if we let it, but if we continue exploiting everything, we will be left with nothing.

We have reached a term airline pilots call '*cognitive Incapacitation*'. Mental overload and mental fatigue are two degraded cognitive states that are known to promote **cognitive incapacitation**. We see the realities of what is around us but we fail as a global planet to change what we are doing, because we are overwhelmed by our own lives and an overloaded with misinformation by those that deny the reality of our circumstances. Therefore, we are paralyzed to do what is necessary to avoid planetary disaster. We are so paralyzed and overwhelmed with all that is required to be done we are frozen to do nothing. Insanity is doing the same thing over and over and expecting different results. That witticism is usually attributed to Albert Einstein.

We somehow live in denial and that somehow things will change for the better. We cannot see that our life styles are the cause of a deteriorating planet; we just do not see the connection and therefore are in denial.

"*Give man a fish and you feed him for a day. Teach a man how to fish you feed him for a lifetime.*" Unfortunately we forgot to tell him not to catch every single fish and then poison the water with chemicals and plastics.

Chapter 15
Global Conscience

The goals are enormous we must start one step at a time to achieve global consciousness.

This is the time to seize the moment '*Carpe Diem*'. It is time to explore who we are, how we can be of benefit to the planet not to its detriment. To enhance what we are to be in total enjoyment of life around us, by enabling all life. Life is all interconnected on this planet when we take away a species, an insect, a plant it unravels with unknown consequences. When we built dams did, we want knowingly to not allow fish to swim upstream to spawn? No, we were just thinking we will make electricity and save water, now there is little water and little fish. Did we think we would leave people downstream dry? No, we did not realize the global catastrophe caused by global warming. When we do one thing in nature, it unravels other interconnected life on this bio sphere.

Human experience comes from within ourselves, yet we have lost our inner selves, we cannot live our daily lives. Yet we continue to try to manage the world. How can we? When we have not managed ourselves yet we are trying to manage the planet. What a disaster! We have lost touch with reality; we no longer see things as they are. Global warming is upon us; the planet is changing faster and faster, creating disaster after disaster. Yet we continue to try to manage the world nation by nation. What a disaster! We have lost touch with reality we no longer see things as they are. Every nation sees reality through blinders only thinking of its ideological self. We must act in a responsible global manner to become conscious of our detrimental actions and the disastrous consequences for all.

We know global warming is upon us yet we continue to burn fossil fuel to keep industry going to keep the military going, to keep our cars going, to keep the economy growing. We keep going to work while the planet is burning up and becoming more unstable atmospherically. In 100 years, we are going to destroy ourselves. Yet the planet will go on and become a much better place without humanity for all its other creatures.

Can we not see?

Can we not just admit that we in 200 years have committed the mistake of economic industrialization and just start over? Can we not consciously as a species make an effort to start over by putting nature at the top of our economic platform? Can we not do that? This is what human intelligence is capable of, now we just need awareness to reach a conscious level to change for the benefit of all humanity and the planet we all live on.

People may not know their planet but they know they don't have drinkable water, what a tragedy. The world needs a consciousness of change. The current economic path got us to where we are, but we must re-think our dynamic interaction with this planet, all humanity and all creatures on this planet. We must reverse direction. We cannot allow our pollution to become the end game, it is time to change.

A question is the progress humanity makes. The question is affluence a better life or a worse life? That is the question? Have we created a better life for ourselves or not? Then we must stop and ask another question. Is it better to destroy the planet for our economic benefit or to nurture the planet to our full enjoyment of life?

This generation must act, must change. We are here now! If we do not act the next generation will be worse off than this one. People know what a mess we have created but cannot deal with it. Humans will struggle, and life will expose us to what kind of beings we are. These are challenging times that confront us. That is when and who we are and what we are at this time will define us. Are we a part of the solution or are we the problem, the problem we have created. This is all we need to decide. Everyone needs to take a stand in these challenging times for humanity. You will be part of the solution or part of the problem? We want to be part of the solution. This is very important everyone must make this commitment.

We must focus on enhancing this life by taking care of nature. If you knew the future, despite all our intelligence, we refuse to see the future without any clarity. Confidence without awareness is a manmade disaster. We need awareness and consciousness of everything we do around us. We must understand with our intelligence we are unraveling our world, our well-being. Who told us we are the most significant life? Our intelligence has allowed us to become a destructive creature; we must re-think our role on this planet like we have never thought of it before. We are one; we are all interconnected we can become human beings to the whole planet to each other and to all the creatures and living things on this planet, to the benefit of all humanity.

Responsible citizens are required to act; there is a threshold of possibility upon which we are sitting that if we solve the deteriorating condition of our planet, we can solve poverty. Bring well-being to all people we must act for a world solution; this is the time.

We need to build global policies that include every nation. Lawmakers need to hold industry accountable in perpetrating the global crises.

One of the first things we must do as human beings on this planet is to agree to disagree on religion and political beliefs and conquests. Religion and political beliefs are your own personal pursuit, but it cannot be a global agenda. This must be a very first step, if we do not nations will continue their global struggles. This is our rudimentary beliefs. We believe something we were told. All belief systems were created by man. All books were written by man. We need to let go trying to instill beliefs into other cultures. Only then can we achieve some semblance of global cohesiveness.

We are all interconnected on this planet we can no longer remain isolated one from the other we are too many people affecting too many planetary systems that support themselves, that are failing because of our unrestrained economic pursuits. This must change.

We must dismantle the economic infrastructure. It does not matter, man created it, we can dissolve it and start all over for the benefit of humanity and the planet. How do we improve the lives of all beings and creatures on this planet? If we do not deal with it, we are naïve and unconscious. I do not want to be in the generation of people that knew and did nothing. We want to do the right things for all of mankind and live on a fruitful planet. How do we eliminate all the human suffering? If we have a healthy planet, we can eliminate human suffering.

We enact strong laws to not allow corporations to cause any pollution or destruction. The planet, the environment must be protected and re-energized to allow humanity to continue and be the caretakers of this beautiful blue planet.

"Reexamine all that you have been told, dismiss what insults your soul." – Walt Witman.

Chapter 16
What Do We Need to Do?
World Remediation

The laws of the world must be to serve and protect the Planet-first.

The answers are not straight forward, the path is one of radical change that will not happen overnight, but must revolutionize as humanity comes to a conclusion that it must change. We must absolve all debt and move forward if it does not benefit planetary life-systems we do not do it. We place the planet at the top of our economic model; it must be of benefit to the planet first. We must protect forests, water, air and soils.

The right ideas for world remediation of environmental degradation involve unselfish and compassionate behavior and a deep commitment to preserve the natural world, without a healthy natural environment there will be no humans. The task for humans is to stop destroying the environments that sustain themselves. If we fail the planet will do just fine without humans.

The only certainty is the future must look very different from the past. When we look at air pollution from burning fossil fuel to create energy and electricity, transportation, and industrialization, industrial farming, industrial fishing, methane release from gas wells, the entire concept of industrial countries must change. We are impoverishing the poor countries that only have healthy natural environments. We poison them with our industrialization. Most products that people in industrialized countries use today are turned out swiftly by the process of mass production, by people and robots working on assembly lines using power driven machines or cheap labor in Asia. The Industrial Revolution changed people's ways of life. This change has directly influenced the decline of the environment, as economic theories do not include environmental costs and impacts. It assumed infinite capacity for nature to provide. What a wrong assumption!

"We're finally going to get the bill for the industrial age, if the projections are right; it's going to be a big one: the ecological collapse of the planet." – Jeremy Rifkin World Press Review 30 Dec 1989.

Our ability to understand the planet and its total biosphere has taken giant leaps but world governments and leaders continue to ignore the canary has died in the mine. The canary is our coral reefs, the canary is all the pretty song birds disappearing from our skies, and we are not paying attention. We now appreciate the complex system that interconnects us all, the atmosphere, the oceans, and land ecosystems are all linked and interconnected to support all the life on this planet.

We can no longer think in terms of my country, my nation, my continent. We have to change our consciousness to think beyond borders. We have to think, humanity must come to grips that we are all on this (island) in the cosmos we must all share in the consequence of the future of humanity. The planet must evolve its consciousness. The conscious revolution to attain a sense of universal responsibility, we must work together to improve the planet not impoverish it. We need to develop a sense of oneness for all human beings on this planet. We must disentangle the economic massacre that the dollar has created.

The answer is right in front of us. We work for the benefit of the planet. We give back to the planet. When you work and you are giving do you not feel better about yourself? Your cells will feel better; people will feel good about themselves and what they are doing.

How do we do this, by creating dollars for the planet, to nurture the planet using planetary dollars to rehabilitate the environment. Our current financial system is a house of cards, it must be changed. A world monetary shared by all to the benefit of the planet and humanity, we must treat this planet as a whole it cannot be subdivided, it must be to the benefit of the whole. Climate, the environment must be the top priority of all nations protecting environments for the benefit of the whole. "Planetarianism"

We have many things we need to correct. It is just a new way of looking at the economy.

We change from industrialization to a conscious awakening of our planet. "Conscious Planetary Evolution." called PLANETARYISM. We must bring all pollution under control, water pollution, air pollution, ground pollution.

It is money spent on the well-being of the planet for the well-being of itself, for the survival of humanity.

Companies must make products that do not cause any pollution, and they must be responsible in recycling their products. Everything must be recycled, no more one time use products to be dumped in nature. All chemicals must be certified that it will not kill plants, animals or insects. Why? We poison insects or rats, they get eaten by birds or large animals that are in turn are poisoned, and suddenly we have no birds. Companies can take from nature but must replace the land as it was. If a tree is cut down, two must be planted. If a mine is dug out of the ground, it must be refilled. We must return water ways the way they were. We must stop polluting the air with co2, methane and all other poisonous chemicals and gases. No more proprietary data, companies are guilty unless proven it will not cause harm to the environment.

The world population must decrease. Women who do not have children need to be rewarded. We will institute a reward for them. The best thing for the world is not to add to its population not by building walls so people do not enter into a country. There are too many people everywhere. Countries must agree to decrease their population by 50% through attrition.

We need to change our behaviors we can achieve a lot in terms of well-being and building a healthy society. We need to be happy with what we have and not spend continuously striving for more getting into more and more debt, and continuously being unhappy with what we have. Not enjoying life but working to the bone just so we can manage our lives and never seeing the end. Where did life go?

We must change our agricultural methods. They can be reversed by switching from the use of industrial chemicals to more of a regenerative organic soil management methods. We must give back to the soil. We must change our farming. Farmers need to plant trees, to sequester the water in the ground and increase the water table. Trees help agriculture, they provide nutritional value for the food that is grown, the land will hold more water, and the soil will become richer. Water tables will increase; acres of forest will nurture the planet, provide shade for all, and homes to the creatures that desperately need them. The trees eat up the carbon dioxide, and the soil moisture and soil richness will come back. The large agricultural footprint on this planet must change. Without change bio diversity will not happen. Soil needs organic matter; it is the nutritional value in everything we eat. Remember how great a tomato used to taste, like an apple now they have no taste and less nutritional value. We need leaves from trees, manure from the animals. Agriculture uses over 80% of the world's water. We are scraping the bottom of the barrel taking water to the last drop. Wells are drying up and ground water is not replenishing. The soil is not holding the water it's just running off the land. Trees improve water quality **by** slowing rain as it falls to the Earth, and helping it soak into the soil. They also prevent soil from eroding into our waterways, reduce storm water runoff, and lessen flood damage. They serve as natural filters to protect our streams, rivers and lakes. They breathe in carbon dioxide and breathe oxygen. They change the climate the way we need it. By removing the trees and forests, we are changing the climate the way we don't want it.

Shift our soil from a cause of climate catastrophe to a solution. Because without fertile soil we have no food, without food there is starvation. However, if we do nothing on a global scale if we leave things as they are and do nothing for 20–25 years it may be too late. Then it may take 5000 years to undo what we have done. 1,258,680 hectares of forest cut down or burned per year (January 17, 2022. theworldcount.com.)

The planet can bounce back if we consciously set our minds on doing things differently. It needs to be done now not tomorrow. If we consciously pay attention to the planet if we put back vegetation, lakes that have been drained, rivers that have been dammed, we can consciously turn our blunders into positive conscious thinking.

Are we going to be a responsible generation or not? We must accelerate the process of '*Ecological Transformation*'.

We must enact strong world laws to protect the environment and strong enforcement to enact those laws.

How do we enforce the protection of our precious environment? Armies are used to fight polluters, on the ocean and on the land. Instead of fighting wars they are fighting polluters. Police will no longer intervene when natives protest against oil and gas companies polluting their lands. **We are arresting the wrong people!**

We need to adopt the same intelligence used for aircraft safety.

Similar to (A.I.B.) Aviation Investigation Board or the NTSB (The National Transportation Safety Board) investigates **every civil aviation accident in the U.S. and significant accidents in other modes of transportation**. Based on their investigative findings and special studies, the board makes recommendations aimed at preventing future accidents. Every country has them, they can be created to find accidents in nature and prevent them from happening in the future with recommendations, penalties and remedies. We investigate accidents in nature every country has them. We investigate find and eliminate the cause and publish the results worldwide, with recommendation to avoid future pollution. An example could be the sinking of a nuclear submarine, which is catastrophic in of itself, and would usually not be broadcast because of national interests. It would be treated like an aircraft accident all countries would provide support to recover the submarine with world resources. The submarine is not to be left on the ocean floor when eventually it will break apart and its nuclear radiation will kill all life in the area, killing millions of fish if it is in a very sensitive area. That is just one example. Because we are doing it for the planet it would be covered by the dollars that is owed to no one but the planet itself.

Planes are so much safer because of these different regulatory departments, and each country would govern its own environmental borders, and neighbors' borders, all countries would need to agree to prevent disasters in nature. In fact, it could be part of the UN's mission. "To protect the planet from plunderers and catastrophic accidents" We can enforce this now or do we wait till the earth has suffered enough. If there is a dispute, the UN can rule on the side of nature. We must police our oceans to prosecute against depleting the fishery in the oceans. We are stripping the oceans of life and not replacing it. *"We must have strong laws to Speak for Nature."*

"We need criminal laws that can convict any person or organization that willingly pollutes the environment, our current laws are weak and monetary fines are a joke for multinationals that have billion-dollar profits on the back of our fragile environment."

Chapter 17
The Key 'the Planet Gives It to Us' – Planetaryism

We are at the crossroads, a conscious awakening, and a transformation of enlightened beings that can break down walls. To directly oppose economic structures that cause environmental degradation. We spare no expense for clean air, clean water, clean soil, and a totally clean environment. "The Economy of a Planetary Recovery" called Planetaryism.

How? We change our current economic model to living consciously benefiting all life on this planet.

PLANETARYISM Measure Economic Wealth by measuring the Health of the Environment.

There are hundreds of economic theories the most important ones are taught in universities, but they all lack one extremely important vital component the environment. We need to create a new economy one that directly interacts with the environment. We assign global values for anything the environment provides not subject to market fluctuations or shortages. This small measure will prevent the pillaging of the environment. Food, shelter, medicine, basic human necessities cost need to be frozen by all governments. If all humans have the basic necessities to live life, then wars become unnecessary. We can all live within our means not continuously outstripping the environment.

The debts of all nations and all households are to be forgiven. The concept of money and debt was invented by mankind for the convenience of bartering. It was invented with economic growth as the main stimulus for the economy, uncontrolled economic growth has seen its day, look where it has gotten us, and we need to change. We need to remodel our future by measuring economic wealth differently, by measuring the health of our environment not economic growth. We must move from Communism and Capitalism to Planetaryism.

"Planetaryism" is simply humanity holding the planet as its most important asset and taking care of the planet above all else. If it does not aid the planet, it is not done.

Creation of a new World Money—All activities associated with cleaning the environment, protecting the environment, increasing the wealth of the environment shall be earned from the World Money. The world money is not associated with debt; it is completely devoid of debt. The world money is the quadrillions of dollars required to rehabilitate the environment and is paid by the planet earth to human beings to allow humanity to continue living on this planet.

These dollars directly clean up the environment, plant trees, protect the Amazon, clean up the oceans protect and rebuild the environment, protect wild life, protect rivers and lakes.

We turn our economy upside down with the care of the planet first we make the planet the peak of the economy, the planet and all creatures on it first. It must benefit the planet first. Profit and wealth are no longer the measurement used. We have many things we need to correct. It is just a different way of looking at the economy. We need to completely collapse our economic calamity, and dismantle the economic web of entanglement. The new measurement must be 'The environmental health of the Planet'. If we correct this, the planet will support us if we do not future generations will live very poor lives if at all.

The big question is who is going to pay to clean up the historical mess that we have created? If we continue with our current economic system of unbridled debt, no one will. It is a hole we can never climb out of; we are all trapped. We are trapped in a 'web of entanglement' that freezes us to inaction and incapacitation that only leads to further debt and misery. How will all the money we need, go back to who it came from? It goes back into the well-being of the planet. This is where we need to undo the 'economic entanglement' that humanity itself has created. We must start over. We are the Roman Empire with all its might it came crumbling down, this is where we are.

Who does all the money we are going to use go back to? Who owes it to who? No one owes it. Open up your minds; think out of the sand box we have been caught in for the last 200 years. *"THE PLANET GIVES IT TO US FOR ITS OWN WELFARE."*

We change our economic model from unabated economic consumerism to a conscious planetary evolution, by bringing all pollution under control. It is money spent by the planet for the well-being of itself. We turn our economy upside down with the care of the planet above all other economic decisions. If it does not benefit the planet, we do not do it. If it poisons water, air, soil, plants or animals, we do not do it. This is the key in our new world economy. The economy is no longer measured by economic growth but measured by healthy environments and healthy eco systems, that is where the wealth is and if it is healthy, we will no longer need to work for false promises. Countries that have the lungs of the world are the richest countries like the Amazon. They are given world dollars to protect the Amazon.

We need to create planetary jobs to get our blue planet back to a healthy state. Any job that involves the cleanup of oceans, plastics, planting trees, guarding wild life, protecting forest areas, countries protecting their environment, re-stocking the environment with fish and wild life. We must protect rain forests, water ways, the ocean, fish stocks, natural resources and wild life. In fact, anything that benefits the planet. This is what we need the army and policing for; to protect our natural habitats, not to protect companies that destroy the very health of the planet or fight wars that benefits no one.

Who decides how much of the money is produced? There is no limit to the amount to the amount of money, if it directly helps this blue planet. We help it, it will help us.

A person or company can create jobs that will benefit the planet, a company must show and demonstrate that the work created is to develop or enhance or protect, or clean up and rehabilitate our planet.

We can sell products, we can make profits, but only if we are aiding the planet to get back to where it was before industrialization took us to where we are.

The goal is to live more and work less, but doing work that will benefit the planet and benefit each other and will make us all feel better about one another all helping for a common goal, the survival of our next generations.

PLANETARYISM EXPLAINED

It is a new Consciousness—to protect water, soil, air, plants, trees, and animals.

We must be conscious of our planet move from unconscious humans to conscious beings.

We must be compassionate to all humans, to all animal species, to all plants and trees.

The world is one, the planet is one where land, rivers, ocean, air knows no boundary. People are one and must interact with our environment as one.

We come to the realization that consciousness is everywhere and within all living things.

War is barbarianism. The armies are to protect against wars and protect the environment.

World money policy is created to allocate world funds toward the protection of the environment. The funds are used for the protection and improvement and maintenance of rivers, ocean, soil, air, trees and all wild life. Caveat: World money can only be used for basic necessities—food, shelter, clothes, medical, education. All basic income below the poverty line is topped up with world money. It will free all of us from an existence without poverty.

We listen to Mother Nature; we act in balance with her seasons and planetary migrations. No constructions during nesting seasons, no large-scale constructions during fish migrations upstream. All creatures are in tune with the night and day no lights at night in tall buildings, where millions of birds have been killed. No airline flights during bird migrations. We have totally lost our touch with the planet; we think we can be separate from it, we are not. There is so much more we need to listen to Mother Nature to learn from. There is so much more we need to do.

We need to create strong environmental laws that will severely punish those that that pollute the environment.

We need to have check and balances to ensure that the world money was indeed used the way it said it was, such as armed forces to protect the Amazon, Africa etc.

Provide planetary dollars to countries that have significant rain forests and wild life to protect its wealth.

"Take nothing but pictures. Leave nothing but footprints. Kill nothing but time." – Motto of the Baltimore grotto, a caving society.

Summary

We move from Communism and Capitalism and other types of government, to Planetaryism.

Ecological issues must become election issues. All governments must give significant importance to ecological issues. How do we do this, by changing laws, by becoming passionate toward all Humanity and conscience of our interactions with the Planet, as one humanity.

We move toward adopting new commandments for the planet. In the future, they can be changed as they are not written in stone. 1. Do not pollute the water 2. Do not pollute the soil 3. Do not pollute the air 4. Be compassionate to all people 5. Be aware of the conscience within all animals and species 6. Be aware of all water, plants and trees and their vital importance to the planet. 7. Always be conscious of your life and the life around you on the planet. 8. Only consume what is necessary to live, nothing more. 9. Do not overpopulate the planet. 10. Use power to protect the environment.

"The old Lakota was wise. He knew that man's heart away from nature becomes hard; he knew that lack of

respect for growing, living things soon led to lack of respect for humans too." – Chief Luther Standing Bear.

This is a positive time in the history of Humanity, there is so much work required to rehabilitate our planet. We can employ and feed everyone while we correct the pollutions we have created. We have a lot to do let us get started with a radically different approach to life on this planet.

The world currency will be tied to world health. We will measure economic wealth by the quality of the water, the quality the soil, the quality the air, the quality of the environment, the diversity of species. That is where the richness is. The richest countries will be those that best protect natural environments.

The army will protect the fisheries, the animals, the trees, the environment.

"I think the environment should be put in the category of our national security. Defense of our resources is just as important as defense abroad. Other-wise what is there to defend?" – Robert Redford Yosemite National Park dedication 1985.

This is a positive new beginning that will lead to better lives for everyone on this planet as we are all interconnected.

Millions of jobs will be created, we are at war and we are the enemy. We need people, personnel, manpower and a new found intelligence and consciousness to rectify the environment. We need brain power to re-imagine how to clean up the environment, to mobilize companies in this cleanup effort, get plastics out of the ocean. We remobilized car companies to build planes and tanks during the war, this

211

is war and we can do it. Let us move forward to a new age of planetary consciousness.

Create Planetary Life Skills with dollars to support the planet given to us by the planet.

These are end goals that we must all strive for, we realistically need to start to take the first step toward planetary rehabilitation. It is going to take a conscious effort from the whole planet. Because we are all interconnected it is the raising of human consciousness beyond what we have learnt. We need to re-learn our roles on this planet, all nations together to rehabilitate the planet for future generations. I am sure there are many more goals that can be added.

All governments must focus their laws on the enforcement and protection of the environment. Water, air, soil, forests.

We cannot produce the food we need to feed billions of people. If we do not immediately correct what we are doing, there will be nothing to feed the population. But, if we correct it and resurrect our oceans, our rivers, our farms, our biosphere, there will be plenty for everyone.

This is a life altering change for the whole planet.

In the long run, we will feel good about ourselves and we feel that we are doing something worthwhile for the planet and that we can be proud of the work we do.

It will not be easy change, it never is, but we must if we are to survive as a conscious species, otherwise we are creating the next mass extinction, and we do not see it but it is right before our eyes.

"Something will have gone out of us as a people if we ever let the remaining wilderness be destroyed; if we permit

the last virgin forests to be turned into comic books and plastic cigarette cases; if we drive the few remaining members of the wild species into zoos or to extinction; if we pollute the last clear air and dirty the last clean streams and pushed our paved roads through the last of the silence, so that never again will the people be free in their own country from the noise, the exhausts, the stinks of human an automotive waste." – Wallace Stegner, letter to David E. Pesonen of the Wildland Research Center, 3 Dec 1960.

The world needs to change; Victor Hugo said that 'nothing is more powerful than idea whose time has come'.

Index of Solutions

The 80/20 rule applies to our environmental calamity. The easy solution is to eliminate 20% of industries that cause 80% of our environmental issues.

Stop gas exploration and fracking
Discontinue Stop farming with fertilizers
Discontinue use of coal
Discontinue industrialized size farming
Stop tree cutting and deforestation
Discontinue product obsolescence
stop excessive packaging
Significantly reduce transportation methods
Discontinue co2 emissions
Stop building oil pipelines
Discontinue tar sands
Discontinue chemicals unless proven safe
Control population
Stop building dams
Stop nuclear bomb production
Stop oil exploration on vulnerable eco systems
Protect all water
Stop single use plastics

Stop use of chemical fertilizers

Stop chemical insecticides

Recycle all pills

Rethink global transportation and passenger cars

Outlaw any throw away products

Discontinue over fishing

Stop use of trawlers and industrial size fishing fleets

Discontinue palm oil

Discontinue genetically modified crops

Discontinue oil platforms

Reduce vehicular traffic

Recycle everything.

Epitaph

The future of the planet earth is known. The future is for humanity to create. What will be our choice? Scientific reality has shown us that the current path we are on will only lead to our demise. We must act responsibly as a planetary community for the freedom and prosperity of all humanity to interact in a new conscious reality, in sync with what this planet has, provided that we take care of this planet; our only home and all its inhabitants. We must become the gardeners and caretakers of all life that inhabit this very unique place in the universe. We must open up our consciousness to become aware of our surroundings and all living things. It is this time in the history of humanity that we put all our differences in a trash heap and come to the conclusion we all need to help each other compassionately, to the realization this is our only home, our only world, our only life, our only future.

Why am I here, what is my purpose? We are all here to help this planet survive, to be gardeners and caretakers of this planet and of each other in a caring and compassionate way. That is why our species has been given intelligence; we just need to acquire awareness and consciousness of everything that is around us. All we have to do is leave nature alone, it will heal itself.

Time is of the essence; we have less time than we think. Look up, listen, birds are vanishing; their crisis is our crisis.

We are failing our children. We are facing a humanitarian crisis of epic proportions. If we do not act in a radical way, we as humanity will no longer exist as we will face a total societal collapse in 30 to 50 years. The welfare of each is bound by the welfare of all.

Printed in the USA
CPSIA information can be obtained
at www.ICGtesting.com
LVHW011724180824
788599LV00002B/202